Why God? Jesus? the Catholic Church?

Why God?
Jesus?
the Catholic Church?

JOHN-MARK L. MIRAVALLE

WHY GOD? WHY JESUS? WHY THE CATHOLIC CHURCH?
JOHN-MARK L. MIRAVALLE

All rights reserved.
Copyright ©2014 by John-Mark L. Miravalle

No part of this book may be reproduced, stored in a retrieval system, or transmitted in any form or by any means, electronic, mechanical, photocopying, recording or otherwise, without the prior consent of John-Mark L. Miravalle.

First edition, first printing in USA
ISBN: 978-0-9903966-0-4

To order copies, please visit
www.SchoolofFaith.com

Book and cover design
Suzanne C. Hurtig, www.SuzanneHurtigDesign.com

Table of Contents

Introduction	Faith, Reason, Apologetics, Evangelization	...vii

WHY GOD?

Chapter One	External Proofs for God's Existence	.3
Chapter Two	Internal Proofs for God's Existence	15
Chapter Three	Some Objections to Theism	27

WHY JESUS?

Chapter Four	What's So Special About Jesus?	41
Chapter Five	Reason #4: The Resurrection (Did Jesus Really Rise from the Dead?)	49
Chapter Six	Some Objections to Christianity	57

WHY THE CATHOLIC CHURCH?

Chapter Seven	Why We Need the Catholic Church	67
Chapter Eight	The Church As Jesus' Body	77
Chapter Nine	Scandal in the Catholic Church	89
Conclusion	The Basics of Prayer	97
Appendix	How Do You Know You Have a Soul?	107

Introduction

FAITH, REASON, APOLOGETICS, EVANGELIZATION

WHAT IS FAITH?

The notion of faith is hard to get a handle on initially, so to start let's talk about a very closely related term, namely "belief." What is belief? Unfortunately, in popular usage today, the word "belief" is normally used to indicate an uncertain opinion. "Is it going to rain later on today?" "I'm not sure, but I believe so."

In the technical sense of the term, however, *belief is when you hold something to be true based on the testimony of another.* Belief happens when someone tells you something you couldn't know on your own, and you choose to accept it as accurate. Take the following example: Suppose I've had to leave my wife for a month to go on an extended business trip. Suppose further that while I'm on a long-distance phone call to her, my wife informs me that she's pregnant with my baby, that we're expecting. Now of course, this is information that goes beyond my direct personal experience. I wasn't there when she took the pregnancy test, and I didn't see the test results. But my wife assures me we have a child together, and I decide, I *choose*, to believe her. As a result of my belief, I have increased my own knowledge by sharing in hers; now I know what she knows. And this newly gained knowledge has a massive impact on my life; I have to start making preparations for fatherhood.

This is the beautiful reality of personal communication. We all share knowledge with others, and we depend on them to share knowledge with us. But for this to happen, for communication to actually take place, the listener must make a choice to place his trust in the speaker's truthfulness.

An enormous amount of what we know comes through belief. History is a good example of a field where just about everything you know comes from the testimony of others. But it's also true of most things you learn in school. How do you know the periodic table includes all known elements? How do you know F. Scott Fitzgerald wrote *The Great Gatsby*? How do you know Madagascar exists (assuming you haven't been there)? You can't sit down with pen and paper and prove it, can you? You have to accept other people's word for it. That's belief.

Now faith is a very special kind of belief. *Faith is when you hold something to be true based on the testimony of* **God**. With this theological virtue, God tells the person something he couldn't have known on his own, and that person makes the decision to accept what God says as true. Faith is therefore the virtue that enables us to add heavenly information to our knowledge—we can know what God knows—and this information radically changes our lives.

Believing God

The first aspect of faith regards *Whom* you believe. Every act of belief is primarily an act of trust in the person speaking: it is placing your belief in someone, not just something. Return to the above example of my wife calling to tell me we're pregnant. If I respond to her, "You know, I don't think that's true. Despite what you've told me, I'm pretty sure what you've said is false," well then I'd better get ready for a harsh reception upon my return home. She will be very angry (and rightly so), and will probably say in outrage, "You don't believe *me*?" The point is that belief and disbelief are always personal; it is an acceptance or rejection of the individual as well as the information.

But in the case of faith, it's a matter of personally trusting God Himself. Before we can have faith, God has to speak to us, at which point we'll have the option of accepting His testimony or rejecting it. Somehow or another, He has miraculously communicated to us a knowledge of supernatural things. How did this happen? When did this happen?

Well, it's different for everyone, and for most it's difficult to pinpoint exactly where God offered His Revelation. Usually, God uses some medium to communicate: parents, a friend, a book, a song, a priest's homily. Perhaps your initial moment of faith came as one powerful, instantaneous experience, like when Our Lord called Matthew, and the latter instantly rose up and followed Him. Or maybe it took long years of seeking and listening for the ultimate truth of God, as was the case with St. Augustine. Or it could be that you were brought up in a very devout, Catholic family, which is what happened with St. Thérèse of Lisieux.

Regardless, what's important is that in the act of faith, you believe not because of what your mother or father or friend or parish priest says, but because of what God says. After all, God's the only one who would really know; He's the only one who has first-hand knowledge about the Trinity, the Incarnation, the Redemption of the world, and the beautiful family structure of His Church, and therefore only He can be the source of the Revelation to which we assent in the act of faith.

Our faith, then, rests exclusively on God's authority. *We believe because God said so.* Practically, this means that if your parent or parish priest or confirmation sponsor—or whomever it is that you strongly associate with your faith—does something scandalous, or leaves the Church, it should make you sad, but it shouldn't shake your faith. Our belief shouldn't be based on their testimony, but on God's. Remember the story of the Samaritan Woman, who ran off to tell all her friends about Jesus? She was the initial medium God used to spread the faith to the local villagers, but after they had heard Jesus directly, they said to the woman, "We no longer believe because of your word; for we have heard for ourselves, and we know that this is truly the savior of the world" (John 4:42). That should be our attitude as well to the truths of the Church: God sends many messengers of His truth to us, but we know that truth is founded on a greater source than the messenger.

At this stage it is helpful to consider the principle that *the certainty of your belief depends on the credibility of the witness*. So if somebody is a known liar, you're not going to have a very firm belief in what they say, whereas belief in an honest person is much more secure. But if the person speaking to you is always, by His very nature, truthful—if He is Truth itself, incapable of lies or error—then your belief in what He says can be absolutely certain. And this is, of course, the kind of Witness we're talking about with faith. So it's very erroneous to oppose faith to certain knowledge. Quite the contrary, faith is the most certain knowledge we can have, because it's knowledge that comes from God.

Let's say, for instance, that an archeologist, or a dozen archeologists, declared that they had found the body of Jesus Christ. They claim to have found proof that Our Lord didn't rise on the third day after His death and then ascend into Heaven. Well, that's human testimony that goes directly contrary to divine testimony, which comes to us through the Bible and the Church. In such circumstances, the virtue of faith would recognize that God is more credible, more authoritative, than any or all human experts. So the person with faith would confidently know that—for whatever reason—the archeologists were mistaken. If people say things which contradict what God says, you know the former is wrong. This is the certainty that comes from basing one's beliefs on divine testimony.

What Do You Believe?

Although faith demands placing one's trust in the Persons of the Trinity, that isn't all there is to it. There is an actual *content* of belief, actual things that we must hold to be true. Let's go back yet again to the original example of my wife calling to let me know we're pregnant. Imagine that, after she has announced this wonderful and exciting news, I respond by saying, "Dear, I totally believe you, but I don't think we're having a baby. You're either lying or mistaken and what you have said is untrue. But I totally believe you." Well, of course, such a response would be pure nonsense. My wife (who seems to get angry with me in a lot of these scenarios), would exclaim, "What do you mean you believe me?! How can you pretend to believe me while disbelieving what I'm saying?!"

She would be quite right. If you really trust the speaker, then you accept what the speaker says as true. This is equally required for the theological virtue of faith. Many people try to reduce faith to a mere feeling, a "sense of some ultimate out there." Such a feeling is irrelevant and meaningless on its own; faith remains insignificant unless actual propositions are held as true on God's authority.

The question is, where do we find this content of faith, these propositions which must be believed? Where are they contained? Actually, one of the best places to find the truths of faith is the Creed, which we Catholics say at every Sunday mass. It is called "Our Profession of Faith." In the Creed we declare our belief in the Trinity, in God's becoming man at the Incarnation, Christ's Redemption of humanity through His Death and Resurrection, the Catholic Church, and the Sacraments. This is a good general outline of what God has told us and what we are to hold as true on His authority. A more detailed presentation of the truths of our faith is given in the *Catechism of the Catholic Church*. If you're looking for the specifics of what we believe, that's a great place to go.

What Is Reason?

Throughout these chapters, we're going to be looking at a lot of arguments, at a lot of pieces of evidence that support the Catholic worldview. In other words, throughout these chapters we're going to be doing a lot of reasoning.

Reason is a very basic form of knowledge, the kind of knowledge we get from proofs and arguments, from logic and inference. With reason, we *begin with what is known, reflect on it, and conclude to what was not previously known.*

Now it's important to note that a great deal of what we know isn't something we get from inference/proof/reason. Think again of all the stuff you know regarding history, geography, science, your personal life, etc… Most of the things we know in these areas come either from our own observations or because we received the information from someone else.

That's why it's so irrational, so unreasonable, so unrealistic, to demand proof for everything—because most of the important knowledge we have can't be proven. As Chesterton points out, a lunatic isn't someone who's lost his reason; he's someone who's lost everything else. If you're not going to trust your own experiences, or the testimony of other people, then you can still do math, and a little philosophy, but for everything else the only consistent thing to do is sit in a cell, shut your eyes, cover your ears, and repeat over and over again, "Lies, it's all lies!"

One more thing: We discussed how belief is a very legitimate source of knowledge, and one that shouldn't be dismissed or devalued. But still, isn't it true that whenever our reason/inference clashes with our belief, we should always go with reason?

Actually, no. Not always. In fact, it may be more realistic in a certain situation to accept someone else's testimony rather than the conclusions of your own reasoning.

For example, say you're taking an advanced math class in college. Math has always been one of your weak points, whereas the teacher is known to be an expert in the field. Say you've taken a pop quiz earlier in the week, and today the teacher is handing back the graded quizzes. As soon as she hands yours back, you see that she's marked your first answer wrong. Remember too, that the answer you wrote was the conclusion you reached through a process of reasoning. But she says it's wrong. So, given that you're not very good at math and the teacher is extremely good, is it more realistic to think that you got the answer right or that you got it wrong? If you have any humility—which is a prerequisite for good, realistic judgment—then you're going to assume that the teacher was right, and you're going to recheck your reasoning process.

The same is true for a Catholic in matters of doctrine. Sometimes our reason seems to lead us to a conclusion that contradicts our faith (i.e., our belief in Christ's teaching as it comes to us through the Scriptures and the Church). But in such a case it's more realistic to accept what the Teacher is telling us, even though we might have to do a lot more thinking before we can figure out how to make sense of it from the point of view of our own, modest reasoning.

What Is Apologetics?

Now some things you can know with reason alone, apart from God's special testimony through the Scriptures and the Church. For instance, many non-Christians throughout history have figured out, just by reasoning carefully, that there is a God and that He must be responsible for the universe and that He must be all-perfect. So the first couple chapters will focus on God, and on how we can know Him through reason.

But many of the things we're going to talk about can't be *proven*. These are matters of strict faith: you couldn't know them unless God revealed them. These propositions are true, and, as we saw above, we can have *certain knowledge* that they're true, but we can't *prove* that they're true. Because we didn't experience these things directly. We didn't see Christ rising from the dead, and we haven't yet come face-to-face with the Trinity. Nor can we invent an argument that will logically prove these facts. That's what makes faith so meritorious, so noble: "Blessed are those who have not seen, but believe" (John 20:29).

However, although we can't prove our faith, we can still demonstrate its *credibility*, which is to say that we can show *how sensible it is, how beautiful,* and even *how likely*. Further, we can defend our faith from attack, show that it isn't silly or absurd. When we do this, when we show that the faith is *believable, plausible, not absurd*, we're doing **apologetics**, and it's a great way of removing obstacles to someone's belief. Not only that, but the better we understand the reasons that support our faith, the more intellectual satisfaction we'll have in our own Catholicism.

Sharing the Faith

All the same, it's very, very important that we not make the mistake of thinking that the only way to share our faith is through argument. Apologetics is good for helping to remove a person's confusion about a specific issue, but it's no substitute for actually bringing someone to Christ. Remember, faith means accepting God's testimony, not human inferences. We can't argue someone into the faith; God has to show the person His truth. And that has several important ramifications.

Firstly, if you're dealing with someone who demands a perfect logical argument for the acceptance of the truths of faith, you'll never be able to convince him. Instead, the best thing to say to someone like that is, "Please just pray to God to reveal Himself and His truth to you fully. Open yourself up to what He's trying to say to you. I can't show you the truth of the Faith; He's got to do it. So come and see. But you have to be open."

A great example of this is the story of Philip and Nathaniel:

> Philip found Nathaniel and said to him, "We have found him of whom Moses in the law and also the prophets wrote, Jesus of Nazareth, the son of Joseph." Nathaniel said to him, "Can any-

thing good come out of Nazareth?" Philip said to him, "Come and see." Jesus saw Nathaniel coming to him, and said to him, "Behold an Israelite indeed, in whom there is no guile." Nathaniel said to him, "How do you know me?" Jesus answered him, "Before Philip called you, I saw you under the fig tree." Nathaniel answered him, "Rabbi, you are the Son of God, you are the King of Israel!" (John 1:45–49).

In the story Philip comes to offer the good news of Jesus Christ, and Nathaniel wants to argue about some silly minor issue ("Can anything good come out of Nazareth?"). Philip, though, resists the urge to get into an irrelevant argument, ("Sure good things can come out of Nazareth. They make good tables up there, and have you tried their wine? Very tasty."). Instead, he says, "Come and see." He knows not to waste his time arguing when the best thing to do is just to try to make the person open to meeting Jesus personally. And what's the outcome? Nathaniel is converted.

So if there's somebody who just wants to argue, somebody who likes to go back and forth just for the fun of it, *don't indulge him*. Stop arguing. Invite him to open himself up to Christ.

In fact, as Pope Francis has recently pointed out, **evangelization** (sharing your faith with someone) usually doesn't start with argument. It usually doesn't start with preaching, or proclaiming, or even talking. Usually evangelization should start with *listening*:

> In this preaching, which is always respectful and gentle, the first step is personal dialogue, when the other person speaks and shares his or her joys, hopes and concerns for loved ones, or so many other heartfelt needs. Only afterwards is it possible to bring up God's word, perhaps by reading a Bible verse or relating a story, but always keeping in mind the fundamental

message: the personal love of God who became man, who gave himself up for us, who is living and who offers us his salvation and his friendship. This message has to be shared humbly as a testimony on the part of one who is always willing to learn, in the awareness that the message is so rich and so deep that it always exceeds our grasp. At times the message can be presented directly, at times by way of a personal witness or a gesture, or in the way which the Holy Spirit may suggest in that particular situation. If it seems prudent and if the circumstances are right, this fraternal and missionary encounter could end with a brief prayer related to the concerns which the person may have expressed. In this way they will have an experience of being listened to and understood; they will know that their particular situation has been placed before God, and that God's word really speaks to their lives.[1]

That's a big paragraph, but what it means is pretty simple. We all have to be missionaries. We all have to obey Christ's final commandment to spread the Good News of the Gospel to the ends of the earth; we all have to be committed to sharing the faith with those who don't yet know Jesus and His Church.

But generally the first step in this process is *getting to know the other person*. It's listening to that person, asking questions, getting a feel for where that person is coming from. We need to make sure that person knows that we're interested in him or her—not just that we're interested in showing that we're right.

Only after we have a connection to the other person, only after we know the other person's story and frame of reference, will we know how to

---

1 *Evangelii gaudium*, #128.

share the truth of Jesus. Only then will we be able to say with a real conviction, "Come and see."

And in the course of that conversation, people may have questions for us. There may be something about God, or about Jesus, or about the Church that they don't understand. And that's why we need to be prepared with reasons, with apologetics—not so we can win an argument, but so we can help answer a person's sincere question. That's why St. Peter says, "Always be ready to give an explanation to anyone who asks you for a reason for your hope, but do it with gentleness" (I Peter 3:15–16).

That's what this book is about.

Why God?

Chapter One

EXTERNAL PROOFS FOR THE EXISTENCE OF GOD

In Dostoevsky's novel *The Brothers Karamazov*, two brothers named Ivan and Alyosha, one a believer and one an atheist, get together for a meal. They only have a little time, time they could use to talk about family or love interests or the future, but as it happens they talk about none of these things since, as Ivan declares, "the eternal questions have to be settled first of all." So they talk about God.

We'll start out the same way. Is there a God? This is the first question that has to be settled. All religious claims, all Christian claims, all Catholic claims can be dismissed immediately if there isn't a God. But if there is then these other claims demand our attention.

For a very long time, the Catholic Church has not only declared that there is a God, but that God's existence can be proven without bringing up Jesus or the Bible or any official documents. In other words, there are **proofs** for God's existence, and these proofs can be developed in two ways: first, by looking at the *natural world*, and second, by looking at the *human person*. So what we'll do in this chapter is take some time and consider some ways we can know God's existence by looking at the natural world. In the next chapter we'll see how we can know God's existence by looking at the human person.

Proof #1:
God As the Ultimate Explanation for the Universe's Existence

People like explanations for things. They want to find why something is the way it is. *When something isn't self-explanatory, people look for an explanation until they find it.* Now let's unpack that idea of self-explanatory a little more. What does it mean to say something is **self-explanatory**? Well, it basically describes a situation in which something possesses a feature that it has to have. A feature that a thing has to have is also called an **essential** feature. So an essential feature is a feature a thing has to have to be what it is.

Another term we can use to talk about self-explanatory is the word **necessary**. If something has to be a certain way, if it has to have a certain feature, then we would say it's "necessary" for things to be that way, or it's "necessary" for that thing to possess that feature.

Essential and Non-essential Features: Some Examples

So let's try a few examples. First, imagine I have a pen with blue ink, and draw a blue triangle on a sheet of paper. Now this triangle would have three sides. Obviously. Having three sides is an essential feature of a triangle; it's necessary for every triangle to have three sides. So we don't have to ask about that. But this triangle would also be blue. That's not necessary, it's not essential to it. It's perfectly conceivable that the triangle should not be blue. Therefore, *the fact that it is blue stands in need of an explanation.* It isn't hard to give a preliminary explanation, which is that the ink in the pen was blue, and it gave its blueness to the triangle. But then we could ask the question again, *how did the ink that was in the pen get to be blue?* Well, the ultimate answer to the question *how did anything get to be blue* is found in the nature of blue pigment. Blue pigment is the explanation for anything's being blue. Blue pigment is the chemical compound which reflects light at a certain frequency. Blue pigment is therefore *essentially blue*, since being blue is part of what it is. But that also means that blue pigment is the ultimate explanation for why anything is blue. So by finding something essentially blue, something that *has to be blue*, we've found the explanation for why some things, which *don't have to be blue* (like the triangle), are blue.

Okay, let's try another example. This time imagine that a long string of nails is hanging together in a downward chain, and that each nail is held to the other by magnetic force. Also imagine that if you take one nail off the string, the nail no longer displays any magnetic charge. So each one of these nails has a head and a point. No surprise there; having a head and a point is an essential feature of a nail, it's part of what it means to *be* a nail. But each of these nails is also, as long as it's attached to the chain of nails, behaving magnetically. And that's unusual—most nails aren't magnetic—so magnetism for a nail is non-essential. *Which is to say that it's not self-explanatory and therefore stands in need of an explanation. From where are these nails getting their magnetism?*

You might give a preliminary explanation for the magnetism of these nails by saying that each nail is getting its magnetism from the nail above it on the vertical chain. But that just postpones an answer to the question: where are these nails, as a group, getting their magnetism? The ultimate answer, of course, is to be found in a magnet. There's got to be a magnet somewhere up the string of nails. Why? Because that's where magnetism comes from. A magnet is a physical solid that's internally constituted in such a way as to attract magnetic materials. In other words, it's *essentially magnetic*. Being magnetic is part of what it is to be a magnet. So, in finding something that is essentially, inherently magnetic, we find an explanation for things that don't have to be magnetic, but are magnetic (like the magnetized nails).

The Necessarily/Essentially Existing Source of Existence

At this point we're ready to run the drill with a very important feature: *ex-*

istence. Let's try it with human existence. First of all, is being an animal an essential feature of humans? You bet. Part of what it means to be a human is to have a body, which is what makes us different from, say, ghosts or angels. We necessarily have bodies. But do we necessarily exist? Is existence a necessary feature of being human? No, definitely not. I didn't exist not so long ago, and I won't exist (at least, not as a physical human) once I die. So clearly, I don't have to exist. Then why do I exist? Why do you? That stands in need of an explanation.

Here again, I can give a preliminary answer. My parents, the health of my organic functioning, the regularity of planetary motion; all these things help explain why I exist. But then, why do these things exist? They don't have to exist; it's perfectly conceivable that my parents might not have existed, that my body's health not exist, and that the planets move in an erratic, instead of stable, pattern. So the existence of all these things stands in need of an explanation too.

Well, we can only find an ultimate answer by recognizing a necessarily existing source of existence.

Remember that the explanation for the nails' magnetism was only to be found in the necessarily magnetic source of magnetism (the magnet).

And the explanation for the triangle's blue color was only to be found in the necessarily blue source of blue color (blue pigment).

So too, the only explanation for our existence is to be found in the necessarily existing source of existence. And we usually call this necessarily existing source of existence, "God."

Since God's existence is necessary or essential, it's therefore self-explanatory (remember how we showed that *necessary* and *essential* and *self-explanatory* all pretty much mean the same thing?) But if God's existence is self-explanatory, that means once we realize that God exists, we also realize that we don't need to go looking for an explanation for His existence. Existing is part of what it *means* to be God.

This proof for God's existence is called the **cosmological argument**. It shows that God is the first cause, since a cause is something that gives existence to something else. That's what God does. In fact, He's the original cause, and therefore He's uncaused. So sometimes this argument is called the proof for the **Uncaused Cause**. It's probably the most influential of all the proofs for God's existence. Basically it says, "Hey, all this stuff doesn't have to be here. So why is it here?" And it goes on to say, "Well, since this stuff can't explain its own existence, we have to look for something that can explain its own existence."

Objections to the Cosmological Argument

Of course, a lot of people won't be satisfied with this argument, so we might as well consider some of the more common objections to it.

Objection #1:
We don't need to go looking for a cause for the universe.
The universe is just here, and that's enough.

This objection looks at something that's not self-explanatory and refuses to search for an explanation. But why?

It should always arouse suspicion when someone who's willing to ask questions and look for answers everywhere else suddenly decides they don't want to talk anymore just as things start to get interesting. Imagine a detective who's always very determined to solve every murder mystery. But one day, he comes to a crime scene, and when someone asks what he thinks, he just says, "Oh, who knows. We don't have to look for an explanation. It just happened, and that's the way it goes." We'd start to think maybe he had some personal motivation for not *wanting* the crime to be solved.

It's the same when someone who has a healthy degree of curiosity in every other area—who asks questions and answers them—suddenly decides that this question: *Why do all these things exist? Why does the universe exist?*

doesn't need an answer. We might start to think maybe he has some personal motivation for not wanting the question to be answered.

Objection #2:

Why don't we just say that the universe *has* to exist?

Well, we know the universe doesn't have to exist for two reasons. First, the universe is just the group of all the things that don't have to exist. Things like you and me, planets and elementary particles—all things that come in and out of existence. But if none of the individuals have necessary existence, how could the group have necessary existence? Imagine adding blue rocks into a pile on the table. It doesn't matter how many you add, the pile will never turn green. By the same token, it doesn't matter how many unnecessary things you add together, the universe won't suddenly turn necessary.

Also, we know that the universe doesn't have to exist, because we're pretty sure that the universe had a beginning. Which means that the universe *didn't* exist beyond a certain point in the past. So the universe doesn't have to exist.

Objection #3:

You act as though a thing might not exist, the way a thing might not be blue. So, you say, we have to look for the source of the thing's existence, just as we look for the source of the thing's blueness. But that's silly! You can't talk about a thing that doesn't exist! It doesn't even exist!

This is kind of a silly objection, because you *can* talk about things that don't exist (e.g., unicorns, centaurs, elves). Remember, an *essence* or *what a thing is*, is still knowable even if that thing doesn't have *existence*. Besides, if we couldn't talk about them, how could we even say that they don't exist?

Some things don't exist. And some things which do exist, don't have to. Why do they? Again, the only possible explanation is located in something that has to exist. And this something we call "God."

Objection #4:
Maybe the universe didn't have a beginning, so we don't need to look for something to cause it.

To begin with, there seem to be some major logical, as well as scientific, problems about saying that the universe stretches infinitely back into the past. But even if the universe were temporally infinite, that doesn't answer the question regarding where it came from. The question isn't "How old is it?" The question is "Why is it here at all?" If a ball is suspended in the air in the middle of my living room, and someone says, "What's holding that up?" It's not a good answer to say, "Oh, it's always been floating like that." That gives us no explanation. So too it's a lousy explanation for the universe to make a statement about how long it's been around. There's no sense giving a "when" answer to a "why" question.

Objection #5:
Who made God? Why does God exist?

This question is looking for an explanation for what's self-explanatory.

We've already reached the conclusion that something, (which we typically call "God") exists essentially—based on His own internal structure.

Try it this way. How would you answer these questions:

Where does a triangle get its three sides from?
What is it that colors blue pigment blue?
Who gives a magnet its magnetism?

The way those questions are phrased makes it clear that the person asking them doesn't quite understand what he's talking about.

But it's the same with asking, "Who made God? Why does God exist?"

It is of the essence of a triangle that it be three-sided
It is of the essence of a magnet that it be magnetic
It is of the essence of blue pigment that it be blue
It is of the essence of God that He exist

And...

Just as a magnet can confer magnetism on other things
Just as blue pigment can confer blueness on other things
So too God has conferred existence on other things.

Objection #6:
Do things really even have essential features?

That's a good question, and it has a clear answer.

To get there let's begin by talking about non-essential features. That's a feature something can change and still be what it is. For instance, my dog could change his color, and still be the same thing. But he couldn't change his animality (i.e., turn from an animal into a mineral) and still be the same thing.

Obviously, if things didn't have essential features—features a thing required to be what it was—then everything would only have non-essential features. Which means that a thing could change *all* its features, and still remain the same thing. But if something changed all its features, then it would be a completely different thing than it was before. And it doesn't make sense to say that a thing could become a completely different thing, while still remaining the same thing. So it doesn't make sense to say that a thing could have *only* non-essential features. Everything has at least some essential features, which is why the proof for the Uncaused Cause works.

Summary of Proof #1

We look around, and we see all these things that don't have to exist. So what's the explanation for their existence?

1. If an atheist says there's no explanation, then that proves that his worldview is less complete than ours, since we have a good explanation for something and he doesn't.
2. If an atheist says the explanation for all the things that don't have to exist is itself something that doesn't have to exist, then that proves he doesn't understand the issue. What we need is an explanation for all the stuff that doesn't have to exist, so to bring up one more thing that doesn't have to exist isn't to give an answer, it's to bring up one more thing that needs an explanation.
3. Therefore, the only possible explanation for all the things that don't have to exist is Something that *does* have to exist. And we call this necessarily existing Source of the universe's existence, God.

PROOF #2:
GOD AS THE ULTIMATE EXPLANATION FOR THE UNIVERSE'S ORDER

Our universe displays a great deal of regularity. The way the material world operates displays a consistency and stability that allow us to formulate general descriptions for the sake of prediction. So, for instance, we have the speed of light, the four fundamental forces, the laws of motion; these characteristics of the universe display an incredible amount of order. And, to add to all this, there's no reason to think that the universe has to operate the way it does. We can easily imagine a universe where bodies repelled instead of attracted each other, for instance, or where there was no standard rate of movement for anything.

In other words, why does the universe conform to a specific program? Why is there order instead of pure chaos? Where did the order come from?

Many people are under the impression that, if you just give it enough time, raw chaos will eventually produce something that looks very well organized. One very popular thought-experiment involves monkeys jumping around in a roomful of typewriters. If these monkeys never die, and the typewriters never break, will those constantly jumping monkeys ever produce a compelling and equally long sequel to the novel *War and Peace* (we'll call it *War and Peace II*)?

No, they won't. Chaos can't produce order, and monkeys thoughtlessly hitting typewriter keys won't produce *War and Peace II*. To prove this, imagine you're the immortal person whose job it is to review the transcripts from the monkeys typing. There are only two scenarios in which you find a masterpiece sequel to Tolstoy's novel.

Scenario 1. You go zillions of years, during which nothing but meaningless series of letters ever appear on the paper. Then one day you wake up and check the typewriters and you see on one of them a complete, beautifully written, equal length sequel to *War and Peace*. Well then, you'd know something fishy was up. You wouldn't say, "Well, it finally happened." You'd say, "Wait, what just happened?" You'd know somebody had arranged to somehow smuggle some order into that typewriter room when you weren't looking.

Scenario 2. The monkeys are consistently writing significant work: maybe beginning with simple stories, moving on to short fiction, then to poems, novellas, books on literary criticism, and eventually the long-awaited *War and Peace II* appears. In that case you'd know, first of all, that these monkeys are special monkeys. And, more to the point, you'd know that there was order governing the writing process to begin with—from the outset, you were dealing with more than pure chaos.

Both of these scenarios illustrate that order can only come from order, whether it comes gradually or all of the sudden.

Consequently, given that the cosmological constants, the four fundamental forces, the states of matter, etc..., are all powerfully orderly and predictable, and perfectly suited for the sustenance of life on Earth, the question remains: where does this order come from? It's got to come from somewhere. In other words, there has to be a Source of the order in the universe.

Summary of Proof #2

The way the natural universe behaves is a) **orderly** (regular and predictable) and b) **unnecessary** (there's no reason to think the universe has to behave the way it does).

So what made the universe this way? Again, if an atheist says nothing, that means his worldview is badly incomplete, since he can't explain a very basic fact of our experience.

Whereas we have an explanation: there's a Source for this order. And this Source must be free and intelligent. If He weren't free, then He'd *have had* to make the universe this way, in which case the workings of the world would be necessary. But since the workings of the world aren't necessary, (as we saw, we can easily imagine a scenario in which our universe behaved very differently than it actually does), this Source must be free. Also, this Source must be super-intelligent, since otherwise how could He organize a system as complicated as the universe?

So there's an Intelligent and Free Source of the Universe's Order, and we call this Source, "God."

Chapter Two

INTERNAL PROOFS FOR GOD'S EXISTENCE

Alright, now it's time to move on to some proofs for God's existence that can be drawn from human experience. We'll see how God's existence can be shown from two basic human experiences: a) moral insight; b) longing for happiness.

PROOF #3:
GOD AS THE EXPLANATION FOR MORALITY

It's a very simple fact that all human beings have moral convictions. We all know that it's wrong to torture children for pleasure. But then the question is, *how do we know that?* Where did we get our moral convictions? From whom or from what? Well, let's consider the alternatives:

Observation of the Natural World—Not the Source of Moral Convictions

If we want to know what *is the case*, we tend to investigate. We can look around, examine, observe. So why can't we do the same thing when it comes to what *ought to be the case*?

Thomas Aquinas said that our basic moral insights are indemonstrable—we don't get them from other, more basic principles. David Hume said something similar when he said that you can't logically get an "ought" from an "is." What did these two very different thinkers mean?

Well, probably what they meant is that you can't get your convictions from the facts of life because the facts of life frequently go against your moral convictions. The way things are doesn't line up with the way things should be. Our moral convictions tell us that child torture *should never happen*, but our knowledge of the world tells us that child torture *does happen*. So the world can't be the source of our moral knowledge, because the world doesn't present us with a moral picture. We measure the world against a moral standard and find the world wanting; but then where do we get the moral standard?

Our Preferences/Desires—Not the Source of Moral Convictions

Is "an individual's moral convictions" just a fancy way of saying "an individual's preferences/desires"? Surely not.

First: When making moral statements, we insist that the truth of these moral statements is independent of our own personal situation. If someone is torturing children, and we tell him to stop, he might say, "Why? Don't you like it?" We'd say, "Of course I don't like it, but that's not the point. I don't like peanut-butter-and-mustard sandwiches, but I wouldn't say it's wrong to eat them. I'm telling you to stop torturing children, not because I have a problem with it, but because it's sick and it's wrong and you mustn't do it."

Second: We have no tendency to universalize our own likes or dislikes. I powerfully dislike peanut-butter-and-mustard sandwiches, but it doesn't bother me if everyone else wants to eat them. By contrast, it bothers me if *anyone* tortures children, because that's objectively wrong. So we apply morality to everybody, which shows that it's not the same as a personal preference.

Third: I experience *indignation* when something goes against my moral convictions, and I experience *disappointment* when something goes against my desires and preferences. But I don't necessarily experience them at the same time. If I have a craving for cookies, but there aren't any in the cookie jar, I feel disappointed, but I'm not indignant—I don't think something evil happened. So since I have one experience for something going against my preferences/desires, and a *different* experience for something going against my moral convictions, it proves that my preferences/desires are *different* from my moral convictions (since I have a different experience when each one is present).

Fourth: No one ever tries to support personal likes or dislikes with argument. I'd never have an argument with someone about whether I like or dislike peanut-butter-and-mustard sandwiches—and nobody would challenge my claim. There's an ancient Latin maxim, *de gustibus non est disputandum*, which means, *there can be no argument over personal taste*. But we argue all the time about moral issues, which shows that our moral convictions aren't just personal tastes, preferences, or desires.

Survivability—Not the Source of Moral Convictions

Is "this is a good action" equivalent to saying, "this is an action that promotes physical survival"?

Definitely not.

We don't ever justify our actions by saying, "Well, it was in my best interest." We wouldn't laud someone as morally good who needs a kidney transplant desperately, and so kills the first person he finds in order to get a kidney.

In fact, we praise people who give their lives for a good cause, which would be a contradiction in terms if goodness and personal survival were equivalent.

Nor can morality be equated with consciously promoting the survivability of our species or some other species. If I help an old lady cross the street, I don't do it because I perceive some connection between that action and the propagation of humans or arctic foxes. Lots of people have views about what counts as good or bad, even though they've never thought for two seconds about what will promote the survivability of humanity or any other species.

Somebody might say that morality consists in following those impulses which *subconsciously* promote physical survivability. But if it's all subconscious, that means you can't actually know which impulses promote survival and which don't. And then how could you know whether a violent impulse, or an impulse to torture children, promoted survival? And then how could you know the difference between right and wrong? But of course, we do know the difference between right and wrong, and we know it consciously, which allows us to say that some actions are bad and some impulses are unhealthy. So morality isn't something subconscious. It's something we know, and know explicitly.

All of which means that morality isn't consciously about survival and it's not subconsciously about survival. And it's certainly not about following any old impulse that comes along. Next.

Primitive Authority Figures—Not the Source of Moral Convictions

Some people claim that in ancient times, rulers invented the notions of "good" and "bad" in order to get people to do what they wanted. This scenario is really absurd: how on earth did these rulers invent something that they had no concept of? You might as well suggest that a bunch of blind rulers, living in a dark universe, invented the idea of light.

And besides, if people don't already have basic moral convictions, how would "moral language" be of any use in motivating them to do what you want? You can't motivate people by appealing to something to which they're completely insensitive. You might as well suggest that you could motivate a bunch of blind people, living in a dark universe, by promising them bright colors.

So primitive authority figures can't be the foundation for our moral convictions.

Cultural Consensus—Not the Source of Moral Convictions

This theory, sometimes called **cultural relativism**, says that the cultural consensus is what determines right and wrong. It's the culture that comes up with its own standard for what counts as good or evil.

Wrong again.

If this were accurate, it would be impossible to make an ethical comparison of one culture to another, impossible to talk about moral progress in the transition from one culture to another. If each culture had its own ethical standard, we couldn't compare them morally anymore than we can compare the redness of an apple to the taste of an orange.

But we *do* compare cultures from an ethical standpoint. For instance we say that as one culture has succeeded another, we've made progress in our ethical treatment of women, or our treatment of minorities. All of which implies that there is an ethical standard *outside* the cultures that you can use to compare two cultures on any given issue.

Also, if it were true that the culture were the source of our moral convictions, then the very idea of social reform would be a contradiction in terms. Social reform is when you have people, good people, who challenge the cultural consensus. We praise social reformers for doing the right thing in opposing the cultural consensus, which shows that the cultural consensus can't be the basis for our moral convictions.

God: Source of Moral Convictions

So what have we eliminated as plausible sources of our moral convictions?

Well, we've ruled out the natural world, we've ruled out ourselves as individuals, and we've ruled out other people.

What's left?

Seems like the only plausible source of our moral convictions is something—Someone—who goes beyond the natural world, beyond ourselves as individuals, and beyond other humans.

This "Other," this One beyond the world, beyond our own minds and beyond our collective consciousness (whatever that is), this is the one who gives us the knowledge about what's right and what's wrong.

Now what gives this Other the right to tell us what *ought* to be the case? Very simple: this Other made everything, so He knows how everything *ought* to work. God creates the world, and specifically human beings, with a certain design. Some actions fulfill that design, while others impede or frustrate it. God's design for the universe, and specifically for human beings, is sometimes called the **eternal law**, since God willed from all eternity to make the universe and everything in it with the design that it has.

God then graciously bestows upon human beings a more or less hazy understanding of His eternal design. We reflect on this design and, in a more or less hazy manner, recognize which actions will make us become the kind of creatures we were made to be (i.e., good actions), and which actions will make us fail, will warp and pervert our basic structure (i.e., bad actions). So when God bestows this knowledge on us, (apart from any special revelation, like the Bible or the Church or a vision), it's called **natural law.**

That's why everyone has moral convictions, and in a general way there's a very high degree of agreement. Just about everyone accepts that basic principle, *do good, avoid evil*. Then as you get more specific, there's still a lot of consensus. You can ask a bunch of different people, or even a bunch of different cultures, and all of them will agree with the following:

Indiscriminate sexuality (*lust*) is bad.

Indiscriminate killing (*murder*) is bad.

Indiscriminate falsehood speaking (*lying*) is bad.

Indiscriminate property taking (*stealing*) is bad.

Indiscriminate material desire (*greed*) is bad.

Courage and generosity and self-control and loyalty are good.

Not surprisingly, the more specific you get, the more disagreement you're going to find. Some people see the human design more clearly than others, which affects how clearly they can perceive the truth about a particular moral issue. The details are hard to see.

Of course, in Revelation—in the Incarnation, in the Scriptures, in the Pope's infallible teachings—God not only reaffirms the natural law, but also spells out the implications of our design more clearly, and even tells us things about the human design we couldn't have known on our own. When He does this, when He tells us moral truths through Revelation, it's called **divine law**.

But even apart from faith, it's a fact that everyone has moral convictions, and as we've seen we hold a lot of them in common even if we tend to disagree about many particulars. And there's only one explanation for these convictions. The explanation is that Someone has designed the world and designed us too. And this Someone, God Himself, has given us an insight into that design, so that we can start to live well, so we can begin to become the people He made us to be.

Morality only makes sense if human beings have a purpose, and having a purpose only makes sense if we were given that purpose by a Person who knew what He was doing (He had to know what He was doing when he gave us purpose, or else He would have made purpose, but not on purpose, which is absurd).

Put it another way: we all recognize that if something hasn't been made by someone for some purpose, then there's nothing it's supposed to be and nothing it's supposed to do. For instance, my son likes to paint, but I can't always tell what it is he's painting. Suppose I came home one day and saw on his desk a piece of paper with fresh paint on it. I might say, "Oh, what's this supposed to be?" He might say, "Actually, I just spilled that paint on the paper by accident, so it's not supposed to be anything." Or suppose I'm out in the shed sawing something. My son might come out and say, "Dad, what's all this sawdust for? What's this sawdust supposed to do?" Now, since the sawdust is an unintended byproduct of some other process, I'd say, "Well, actually it's not really for anything. It's not really supposed to do anything. So I guess you can do whatever you want with it."

Again, the point is that unless something has been made by someone for some purpose, there's nothing it's supposed to be, and nothing it's supposed to do. But ethics—and all value-language—is where we talk about what *human beings* are supposed to be, and what they're supposed to do. Which means we have been made by Someone for some purpose, and that Someone we call God.

Sometimes people will ask, "What if God told you to do something evil?" But that isn't possible, since it means God would be working against Himself. He'd have made His creatures to fulfill a certain design, and then He'd be working to frustrate His own design. Not very likely, especially for an Absolutely Perfect Being. (In fact, it's logically impossible for something to be given the purpose of failing to achieve its purpose. Which means God couldn't do it.) No, it's precisely through showing us our own design, the design He gave us, that God gives us natural moral principles. He's not going to contradict Himself by giving us a special revelation with an order to frustrate the design He Himself wants fulfilled.

Does all this mean that someone who doesn't believe in God can't be ethical? Certainly not. You can benefit from someone without knowing that person exists. My little daughter, Stella, eats meat and vegetables without knowing about the existence of butchers and farmers. She lives off foods that come from people she knows nothing about. In the same way, people can live off their moral convictions without realizing that those convictions come from God. All the same, as my daughter matures she'll learn about where food comes from, and we pray that as atheists mature, they'll learn about where moral convictions come from, and have the honesty to acknowledge and thank the Moral Source.

PROOF #4:
GOD AS THE SATISFACTION OF THE UNIVERSAL DESIRE FOR PERFECT HAPPINESS

Everybody wants to be happy. As St Augustine said so long ago, that's the one thing everybody can agree on: we all want to be happy. **Happiness**, *the complete satisfaction and fulfillment of the human person* is what everyone, deep down, is really looking for. So how can you get it?

Actually, to answer that question, it's probably best to start with what complete happiness *isn't*. Once we eliminate all the wrong answers to the question, "What can make me perfectly happy," we'll be better situated to see where you can find the true supreme good.

For starters, the supreme good can't consist in **external created goods**. These are all the good things in the world that lie outside us, but which we desire to some degree or another. They aren't states of the body or the soul, but we want them for some physical or psychological reason. Things like *wealth, power, food, exercise, fame, etc...* would fall into this category.

Wealth and power, for instance, can't be supreme happiness. Wealth and power are only valuable as *means*, that is, insofar as they can get you something else. That's why human money and power exist in the first place, is to be means to other ends. There's nothing intrinsically satisfying about money and power. Imagine if I said, "I have the power (or the money) to end world hunger." You'd say, "Oh really? Then why don't you go ahead and end world hunger?" It would be nonsense for me to say, "No, I just like having the power to do it." Again, the point is that power is meant to be used as a means for obtaining or maintaining some other good.

Ultimately, no worldly external good can be complete happiness, since complete happiness is intimately tied to a good life. But external goods are not. Evil men can have plenty of external goods, but we don't consider them perfectly fulfilled or happy. Which shows that you need other things *besides* these external goods to be completely satisfied. Also, perfect happiness could never cause us harm, whereas with external goods, goods like food or money, you can have "too much of a good thing." Look at how Marilyn Monroe's fame contributed to her destruction, or Hitler's power made him a worse monster than he would have been without it.

All of which shows that perfect happiness involves a perfection of the human person *himself*. Since external goods, by definition, all have to do with what is outside a person, and usually with things he has little control over, they cannot be the foundation for total fulfillment.

What about **bodily perfection**—could that be where we find the supreme good? It's amazing how many people think this is the goal of human life, to achieve peak physical condition. They think if our bodies are satisfied—if we're in great shape, eat well, and enjoy vigorous sex lives— we'll be completely satisfied.

But of course we've said that happiness is the total fulfillment of the whole person, which means we won't be satisfied if only our physical component gets what it wants. And it's quite apparent even from the most superficial observations that the person with the healthiest physique isn't necessarily the happiest. Professional athletes, who have everything anyone could ask for from the physical side of things, often live tragically frustrated lives.

Finally, what about our own **soul**? Many people seem to believe that the soul, or the Self, already possesses everything needed for happiness. They think the trick is learning how to tap into the soul's resources, and then we'll find we'd possessed what we wanted all along. You hear phrases like, "I have to discover myself," or "Once I find myself," or "I just need to accept myself for who I really am." Sometimes self-help gurus will say things like, "Everything you need is already right there inside you. You just have to realize it." Could that be true?

No. Definitely not. We all experience, deep within, a desire for more than what we are. The soul desires what is outside of it; it desires truth that it does not know, and it desires good that it does not possess. The human person is not enough for the human person, which is why it's so awful to feel lonely. We long desperately for something more than what we are. We sometimes hear the term "self-satisfaction," but really, there's no such thing as being satisfied with just yourself.

Only God Is Enough

So the soul isn't enough, the body isn't enough, and the good things in the world aren't enough. What is enough?

Why is it that we human beings are always a little restless?

Why is it that we want so desperately to believe that those we love—say, our children, or our romantic interests—are perfect, and then we're so disappointed when they're not? What gave us this desire to be in a loving relationship with a perfect Person?

Why do we want so much to be happy? To be perfectly and permanently happy, even though we know that in this life perfect and permanent happiness is offered to no one?

Usually, when we have a basic urge, there's something that corresponds to that urge. Eating corresponds to hunger, drinking corresponds to thirst, friendship corresponds to loneliness, sleep corresponds to fatigue.

What corresponds to our basic urge for happiness? What corresponds to our basic urge for a perfect relationship with a perfect person? What corresponds to our basic longing to fully understand the world and our place within it?

Even non-believers recognize the human desire for the divine. Many atheists report the illogical—but understandable—anger at God for *not* existing! Sartre, the famous French existentialist, acknowledged that human beings long for the divine, but since he believed there is no God he also believed that humanity is doomed to frustration.

Philosophically, isn't it more reasonable to presume that, since every other urge has the possibility of satisfaction, our urge for the divine has the possibility of satisfaction? Isn't it more sensible to presume that God exists, and that it's possible for us to attain Him? Isn't it more realistic to believe in happiness than not to?

Chapter Three

SOME OBJECTIONS TO THEISM

Now that we've been over the proofs, let's spend some time looking at a few of the more common general objections people employ in support of atheism.

Q. I don't believe in God because I'm a materialist.

A lot of the time people who define themselves as materialists aren't really even sure how to define "matter." They say matter is all they believe in, but then what does that mean?

Does it mean they think only subatomic particles exist? If so, that means they don't even believe in materialists (since a materialist isn't a subatomic particle)—and they don't believe in materialism (since materialism isn't a subatomic particle)—which means they don't even believe in their own view.

Does it mean they think only particles or groups of particles exist? That they don't believe in anything they can't detect with their senses? That anything they can't touch, taste, hear, see or smell isn't real? But does that mean they don't believe in energy, or gravity, or in other people's feelings? After all, you can't detect those things with your senses, but we believe they exist because we see the effects they have. And though we can't see God we believe in Him because we see His effects.

Does it mean that they only believe in what scientists study? But then who counts as a scientist? After all, the word "science" comes from the Latin word *"scientia,"* which just means "knowledge." And there are lots of different kinds of knowledge: knowledge of history, knowledge of literature, knowledge of stars, knowledge of biology, knowledge of mathematics, knowledge of logic, knowledge of geography, knowledge of God. What's your rational test for determining which kinds of knowledge are bogus and which kinds are legitimate?

Does it mean that they only believe in principles they can use to predict the future? But some kinds of knowledge aren't like that. For instance, when we discover the killer in a murder case, it may not help us predict anything two weeks out. But it does tell us something interesting—it helps us make sense of what has already happened. Many people are so busy trying to predict the future, that they don't pay any attention to trying to understand the present. And you need to believe in God to be able to make sense of the present.

Q. I don't believe in God because I think experimental observation and technology will eventually be able to explain everything and provide everything without God.

Better observation will tell us more about the world, but learning about the world doesn't mean changing the world. Experimental observation will give us an increasingly detailed picture of the physical universe, but developing more sophisticated equations and more precise models won't change the fact that the physical universe isn't necessary—and because it isn't necessary it can only be adequately explained by something that is necessary. So advancements in the physical sciences can do nothing to undermine Proof #1.

The same goes for Proof #2. Experimentation and better conceptual structures may give us new information about light, but it won't ever make the nonsensical claim that light is caused by dark. So too new discoveries may show us new aspects to the universe's order, but it will always be nonsense to say that order is caused by chaos. So the fact that the universe is organized will always require an explanation, and the only adequate explanation is to say that the universe is organized because Somebody organized it. Which is why Proof #2 will always work.

Again, physical observation shows us what *is* the case in the natural world. Conducting studies or making more powerful microscopes and telescopes will only tell us about the way things *are*. But since morality is about the way things *should be*, about what *ought to be* the case, we're going to have to look beyond what the natural world shows us if we want to make sense of morality. And beyond the natural world is the supernatural world, which is why Proof #3 for a Supernatural Source of morality has nothing to fear from advancements in the natural sciences.

What about technology? Could technology eventually solve all our problems, give us perfect health and happiness and immortality? Could technology make hope in God and Heaven irrelevant? No, it couldn't. Technology is a tool, and so it's only as good as the people who create it and use it. Technology in the hands of good men has good effects (agriculture, medicine, communication) but in the hands of bad men it has bad effects (weapons of mass destruction, torture devices, computer viruses). So in the hands of imperfect people technology will have imperfect effects. And since everybody's imperfect, technology will always have imperfect effects, which means technology can't make the world a perfect place. And that means our desire for perfect happiness can only be satisfied by God and Heaven, as Proof #4 shows.

> Q. I don't believe in God because if there were a cause of the universe, then that cause would have to exist earlier than

> the universe. But time (along with space) has only existed as long as the universe itself has existed. So nothing could have existed earlier than the universe. So there can't be a cause of the universe.

That's a pretty complicated objection, but fortunately the answer is pretty simple. The answer is that *a cause doesn't have to exist earlier in time than its effect*. For instance, think of what happens when I pick up a pen and hold it in the air. Now my hand's position is the cause of the pen's suspension. But it's not as though I raise my hand and *then* the pen rises into the air. The two events, cause and effect, happen simultaneously. This shows that it makes perfect sense to say that God causes the universe without existing *earlier* than the universe. It's true that "earlier" is a temporal word, so we don't want to say that anything exists "earlier than time." But we also believe that God exists beyond the temporal continuum, that He's not restricted by the limits of time—or space, for that matter. So we can happily say, with no logical fudging, that God exists "outside of time," but not "earlier than time." And because God exists outside of time and space, He can be the cause of time and space.

> Q. I don't believe in God because I don't think you can really ever know anything.

This objection is an expression of **skepticism**, *which doubts that the mind can conform itself to the way things are.* Skepticism is therefore an attack on truth (since truth is when the human mind does correspond to the way things are). Skepticism usually places a divide between a) what's inside our mind, and b) what's outside our mind, and then goes on to say that since we're stuck inside our own minds there's no way we could ever know the way anything is outside our minds. It basically says, "All you can know is what's in your own mind; but that means you can't ever know what's outside your mind. Which means you can't ever know whether your own thoughts are true."

Now we can offer various answers to the different forms of skepticism out there, but I think there's one simple answer that refutes them all. That answer, that refutation, takes the form of a question:

*How did we ever come up with distinction between **truth** and **error** if the mind can't correspond to the way things are?*

Whenever we talk about error, it indicates that somebody isn't seeing things the way they are. But that presumes that at least sometimes, we do see things the way they are (truth).

If our thoughts and perceptions were always distorted, why would we have ever articulated the two categories of truth and error in the first place? Why would we have said that some sensations or ideas were right, and some were wrong? We would have been much more likely to just say, "I see what I see. And I think what I think."

You can only understand something when you understand what it isn't. A blind person doesn't understand what we mean by the word "dark," and a person who can't hear anything doesn't know what we mean by the word "quiet." The reason we know what darkness is, and what we mean by the word "dark," is that we have some experience of its opposite, namely, light.

You can do the same thing with lots of other words. We know what "right" is because we know what "left" is. We understand each of them by mutual contrast. The same goes with male and female. If every animal on earth was male, we wouldn't go around saying, "Hey, we're all men!" ("Men" as opposed to what?)

The point is that if we have a word for "dark," it presumes that we have some experience of the opposite, namely, "light." So too, we know what the word "error" means, because we have some experience of truth.

So we can't say that everything is a hallucination, because if it were *then how did we ever come up with the distinction between hallucination and accurate perception?* We only know what hallucination is because we have accurate perceptions that we can contrast it with.

And we can't say that we just make it all up as we go along, that we just impose our arbitrary constructions on experience, because if that were true *then how did we ever come up with the distinction between truth and fiction, or between real creatures and mythical creatures?* If all our ideas about things are made up, then why did we ever bother distinguishing between things we made up and things we didn't? We only know what fiction is because we can contrast it with reality.

In the same way, it doesn't make sense to say that all we know is what's in our own mind. If all we knew were our own ideas and sensations, *then why do we call some of those ideas and sensations true, and others false?* After all, what's in our head is in our head. The only thing that could possibly make the stuff in our head true or false is whether or not it matches up with what's *outside* our head.

So these forms of skepticism don't really hold up. Everybody knows there's a difference between true and false, accurate and inaccurate, right judgment and error, and that we're capable of knowing the truth. And because we're capable of knowing the truth, we have the obligation to strive after it.

Of course sometimes you meet a skeptic who's really gone the whole way into full-blown **relativism**, *which says that there is no objective reality, and therefore no such thing as truth and error.*

So when you ask a Relativist, *Why do we have a distinction between truth and error?*

He just answers, "I don't believe in truth and error."

You might press the point and say, *But if there isn't any truth and error, why did we even come up with the words "truth" and "error"?*

If the Relativist is really consistent, he might just say, "The answer to that question, as to all others, depends on your preference."

You feel like you're running out of options, but you have at least one more move. You say, *But wait, if there is no truth, then Relativism isn't true.*

Of course, the Relativist might reply, "Sure, whatever you want!"

By now, you're starting to get a little burned up, and you say with some frustration, *But you're contradicting yourself if you're affirming something and then saying it isn't true!*

The Relativist laughs this off like he's laughed off everything else, "Oh, am I? Well, that's okay with me. I always thought contradictions were kind of fun anyway."

You make your final stand, *But when you're affirming something and then denying what you affirmed, it means that not even you believe what you're saying.*

He says, "Well, if that's how you feel, then good for you."

At that means it's time for you to stop talking. If a Relativist takes it that far, it means he's not interested in pursuing the truth anymore. It means he's shut the eyes and stopped the ears of his mind, so that there's nothing more you can do to reach him. Your best bet at that point is to pray for a miracle, pray for God to break through his voluntary blindness and deafness, so that he can see the truth of God, of reality, before it's too late. But there's nothing you can do for him rationally. He's proven that he's not open to clear thinking.

Q. I don't believe in God because in my opinion evolution really explains everything already.

Well, that opinion is really ludicrous because of course evolutionary theory doesn't even *attempt* to explain the origin of the universe, or why the behavior of inanimate matter is stable and orderly and conducive to life.

Also, although evolution may explain a great deal of the biodiversity on our planet, it definitely can't explain where life came from in the first place, nor where intelligence came from.

Why not? Well, because nothing can give what it doesn't have. I can't give you a billion dollars because I don't have a billion dollars. So too, a cause can only give what it already has to the effect, and what's in the effect must have been somewhere in its causes first. That's why, as the great philosopher-priest Fredrick Copleston stated, "If you add up chocolates you get chocolates after all and not a sheep." Chocolates can't produce a sheep, because chocolates don't have what a sheep has (like life, or the powers of sensation), and so chocolates can't give sheep-properties to their effects.

But by the same token, mere minerals, which don't have life, can't produce life. So living things *can't* be caused by non-living things. And irrational creatures, which don't have reason, can't produce rational creatures (humans). So humans can't be caused by irrational animals.

Remember, what's empty can't fill something else. Which means that something devoid of life can't give life, and something devoid of intelligence can't give intelligence. This is where one needs to be very careful in analyzing certain evolutionary claims. If we want to say that on earth life came chronologically *after* not-life, that's fine. And that on earth intelligence came chronologically *after* non-intelligence, that's fine too. But whatever caused life and intelligence to come on the scene must have already possessed life and intelligence.

So be careful when people say that life "emerged" from mere matter, or that human reason "emerged" from lower organisms. The word *emerge* just means "comes out of." It doesn't mean "is caused by" or "is explained by." For instance, a rabbit emerges from a magician's hat, but the magician's hat doesn't produce the rabbit. The rabbit came from someplace that already had rabbits.

In the same way, intelligent life may "emerge" from inanimate matter, but the inanimate matter doesn't produce intelligent life. Intelligent life came from someplace where there was already intelligence and life. Which means we need a primordial Source which itself has life and intelligence.

> Q. I don't believe in God because if He were really there He would show Himself to us.

Well, as we've seen from the proofs for God, God *does* reveal Himself through the natural world and through our human nature. Also, as we'll see in the coming chapters, God reveals Himself through Christ and the Church as well.

But it is true that God doesn't reveal Himself to us directly, in His full glory, in this life, and to understand why we should take a moment to talk about human will and human freedom. Now, just as the mind is the dimension of the person that seeks to know the truth, the **will** is the dimension of the person that *seeks the good*.

However, since there are so many good things in the world, and since we can recognize *some good aspect* in just about everything, the will can choose which good it will pursue. In other words, **freedom** comes from the fact that every possibility has something satisfying about it.

But that's only half the story. The other half is that every possibility has something *unsatisfying* about it. Every good thing has a price, even if the price is not pursuing some other good thing. So we can choose between all these things in the world, because everything is to some degree satisfying, and to some degree unsatisfying.

Now if the mind could perceive that something was totally satisfying, totally desirable, with no displeasing aspects at all, then the will would have to choose that. That's very interesting, because it explains why it is that God hides Himself from us. Why it is that He makes it in some ways unpleasant and sacrificial to choose Him—because that's the only way we have a choice. If we could really see God as He is, if we could really see how possession of Him is really all joy and no loss, then we wouldn't be able to resist Him. Nothing else could compete, it wouldn't have any attractive pull. God has made us free, but the condition of that freedom is that we don't experience Him as He is until *after* we've made our choice. Let's pray we make the right one.

> Q. I don't believe in God because a good God wouldn't make a world filled with evil.

Well, obviously, if God is perfectly good and moral, as the proofs show Him to be, then He couldn't have made a universe that was defective—riddled with pain and corruption. And of course, Judeo-Christian teaching is that He didn't. He made a completely good world. Very good, in fact.

But when God created the world, he had two decisions He needed to make:

Decision One: He could make a world without free creatures, or a world with free creatures. If He made a world without free creatures, then everything would be safe. Nothing would go wrong, everything would go exactly the way it should. On the other hand, there wouldn't be any real love, any heroism, any freedom to choose the good without being compelled. Whereas if He made a world with free creatures, then all of these beautiful things would be possible. But there would be the risk, the risk of creatures failing to choose rightly. If one is free to choose what is good, then by implication one is free not to choose what is good. And if one failed to choose the good, that would mean evil entering the world. In other words, a universe with free choice was a higher-stakes enterprise—there'd be more to gain, but there'd also be more to lose. God chose the higher-stakes universe, and there was free choice, and it was good.

Decision Two: God could make a world without community, or a world with community. In other words, God could make a world where every human being lived on his own separate planet, and where what one person did had absolutely no impact on any other person. Or God could make a world with community, a world of human interdependence, where I depend on you and you depend on me, where part of my role in this life is to help and support you, and vice versa. Now community makes life a bit more intense. For instance, life has gotten more intense since I got married; my joys as a family man are much more ecstatic then they were when I was single, but it's also true that the things I've suffered have been much more painful. That's what a loving community does: it exposes you to greater joys and greater sorrows. In other words, it raises the stakes. Again, God chose the higher-stakes universe, and there was human interdependence, and it was good.

But once human beings are a) *free* and b) *connected to one another*, then if one person freely chooses evil, all the people he's connected to will suffer. That's what interdependence means: if I depend on you doing your part, and you fail, I'm going to suffer—even if I'm innocent. There's no other option: either people are free and interconnected, or they aren't—and if they are, then they can do evil and hurt each other.

And that's precisely what we did, and what we still do. That's what sin is: it's a failure to choose the good which causes a crack in the human condition that cuts through the whole human community. According to the Book of Genesis sin began with our first parents, and obviously sin is still committed today. It is sin—the act of a free creature that brings evil into the world—that is responsible for the physical, psychological and spiritual disorders of the human condition. Sin—whether our sin or someone else's—is why we have trouble adjusting to our environment, why we get sick and die, why we have emotional problems and psychological baggage and why we so often feel far from God.

Obviously a perfect God wouldn't introduce evil into His creation, and obviously people do bad stuff all the time. So it doesn't have to be a big mystery as to where evil comes from: it comes from us.

Still, why would God *allow* evil in His world? Well, we've just given one answer, namely, out of respect for human free will and interdependence.

But there's another answer that completes this first answer. That answer is that God can bring good out of evil, that God can take the sin we freely choose and the suffering it causes—He can take all that and actually use it for goodness and happiness. He can repurpose the ugliness of human life and turn it into something beautiful, the way a great sculptor might recycle a pile of trashy tin cans and turn them into a magnificent metal statue.

How does God do that? How does He harness the mess of sin and suffering and use it in the service of goodness and joy?

He does it in the person of Jesus Christ, whom we'll talk about next.

Why Jesus?

Chapter Four

WHAT'S SO SPECIAL ABOUT JESUS?

So God exists. Good. But now we want to know: has God reached out to us? Can we make contact with Him? The answer to both questions is yes, and the way God reaches out to us, and the way we make contact with Him, is Jesus Christ.

In your average Comparative Religions course at your run-of-the-mill college, Jesus Christ will be presented in a lineup of major religious founders. He'll be there with the likes of Zoroaster, Buddha, Socrates, Confucius, Mohammed, Joseph Smith, and maybe Martin Luther. And the similarities between all these people will be emphasized. They were all persons of strong character, who presented a world-view and preached a moral system. Many suffered for their beliefs, and all of them urged people everywhere to unite in serving a Higher Cause.

The problem is, emphasizing similarities is sometimes more misleading than emphasizing dissimilarities. As C.S. Lewis pointed out, milk and urine are similar in that both come from a cow, but you wouldn't really want to make too much of that similarity when the differences are so much more striking and important.

So too with Christ. It's an enormous mistake to emphasize the similarities between Himself and other religious founders when the differences between Him and them are so much more extreme.

What are those differences? What sets Christ apart? What makes Jesus unique? What's so special about Jesus? Well, basically four things:

Difference #1:
Jesus Was Foretold and Anticipated

If someone is planning on coming to your house for dinner, you'd probably be grateful if they didn't just drop in unannounced. And that goes double for someone important. Think of how agitated you'd be if the President or the Pope knocked on your door without giving you some advance notice.

So if God is going to send someone to Earth to give humanity the secret to the meaning of human existence, it'd be nice to get a little heads up. So which religious leader was anticipated? Which was prophesied? Was Socrates? No. Buddha? Nope. Nobody was expecting Joseph Smith to show up. And Mohammed was a real shock to the region. What about Jesus?

People were waiting for Jesus. People had been hearing about the Christ for centuries. Quite a few details were known about Him before ever He was born. Like:

- **How he would be born**: Isaiah 7 tells us he'll be born of a virgin
- **Where he'll be born**: Micah 5:2 says in Bethlehem
- **How he'll die**: Isaiah 52–53 says he'll die an innocent death, to atone for the sins of many; that he'll be whipped beforehand, and that people are going to cast lots for his clothes.
- **That he'll be a descendant of David** (II Samuel 7:12–14): That may sound pretty easy, but actually Abraham Lincoln had four kids and yet within a few years of his death his line was wiped out. So it's pretty impressive that it was foretold in David's time that one of his descendants would be the universal king, and then many centuries later the line from David to Jesus is still traceable.

- **What the geo-political situation will be at the time:** There are two visions in the book of Daniel, one of beasts (Daniel 2) and one of metals (Daniel 7), and in each one he foretells the following progression of empires: Babylon, Persia, Greece, and Rome. In the time of Rome (which is in both visions characterized by **Iron**), a great stone will fill the earth (the stone which the builders rejected), and one "like the Son of Man" will come and be given everlasting glory and dominion.
- **When that will happen:** Daniel also prophecies that this will occur 490 years after the people are sent back from Babylon to restore the temple (Daniel 9:24–27). And guess who lived about 500 years after Daniel? Jesus.

Oh, and by the way, it wasn't just the Old Testament that talks of this coming Messiah. Listen to these secular testimonies (and feel free to look them up):

Flavius Josephus, the great historian, has this to say in his *Jewish War*: "What did the most to induce the Jews to start this war, was an ambiguous oracle that was also found in their sacred writings, how, about that time, one from their country should become governor of the habitable earth" (6.312–313).

Suetonius, another ancient secular historian, writes in his *Life of Vespasian*, "The old and constant opinion had grown widespread, that it was fated that from Judea would come those who would gain power over all things" (4.5).

Another source, **Tacitus**, writes in the *Histories*: "Most were persuaded that in the ancient texts of their priests it was maintained that in that very time the East would grow strong and that from Judea would come those who would gain power over all things" (5.13).

Aschylus, the great Greek poet, ends his masterpiece Prometheus

Bound by having Hermes, the messenger of the gods, say this "Look for no end of this torment until some God shall come, heir to your sufferings, and choose to enter the sunless realm of Death" (1026–1029).

Virgil, the author of *The Aeneid*, writes what sounds something like a hymn to Mary: "Even now the Virgin returns, and the kingdom of Saturn. Now a new race is sent down from heaven's height. You have born a son who will put an end to the people of iron, and give rise to one of gold all over the world" (Eclogue 4.6–10). Note here how this corresponds to Daniel's two geo-political prophecies about the Christ, both of them stating that He will put an end to the age of iron (=Rome).

Jesus was expected because Jesus was foretold. Wherever he went, everyone approached him and said, "Are you the One? We know Someone is coming; are you He? For we have been waiting." No one was waiting for the others. The whole world was waiting for Jesus.

Difference #2:
Jesus Worked Public Miracles

Before we get on a flight for which we have a reservation, we're asked to show some form of personal ID. They know we're coming, but they want to make sure we're who we say we are.

Jesus Christ has his personal proof of identification as well. It's not a photo ID; it's his miracles. Jesus performs dozens and dozens of miracles, and he uses them as evidence that He's who He says He is. He goes so far as to challenge people: "Believe in me because of the works that I do." Now the most important miracle is the resurrection, and it's so important that we will give it its own chapter, but more generally here are a few remarkable but often overlooked characteristics of Jesus' miracles:

1. He never did a miracle for His own advantage (e.g., when He was hungry He didn't turn the stones into bread).
2. He never did a private miracle.

3. He never did a miracle to satisfy curiosity or popular demand.
4. He never did a miracle that was denied, even by his enemies. Even those who hated him had to admit that his actions were supernatural. The only solution they could come up with was that he was doing his miracles with the help of Satan!

Compare that to other religious founders. Mohammed worked no public miracles. Nor Socrates, nor Confucius. Joseph Smith got tarred and feathered because he said he could do miracles and then failed to deliver. But if God is going to send someone to earth with the message of truth for the world, you'd think He'd give that person the credentials necessary for people to be sure that this was the real deal.

Before going on, though, let's get rid of a silly popular prejudice against the Gospel miracles. Some people will say, "Well, in ancient times, before science, people were willing to believe anything. But now we know miracles can't happen."

But that's manifestly not true. The people in the Gospels aren't expecting miracles around every corner. They act just as skeptical as you or I would act when confronted with the supernatural. When Mary gets pregnant, Joseph doesn't say, "Well, she is pregnant, and it's not by me, but I'm a superstitious Jewish man in first century Palestine, so there's probably some supernatural explanation." Of course not! He may not know modern science, but he knows where babies come from, and he thinks Mary was unfaithful to him. It shows a powerful ignorance of both human nature and the Gospel narratives to act like people were expecting miracles. They weren't. They were as amazed and wary of the supernatural as you and I would have been in the same situation.

Sometimes people say, "There could never really be a miracle, because a miracle goes against the law of nature." But if you believe in God, then a Law of Nature just means the way God usually does things. And a miracle just means when God is doing something unusual. Usually God makes it so that people can't walk on water, but if on occasion He wants to make it so that people don't *sink* when they walk on water, what's to stop Him?

That's why it's very important that we Christians not under-emphasize the miracles of Jesus' life, because if we do we'll be undermining His claims to being really sent from God. Remember when Jesus *physically* heals the paralyzed man, so that we might know "that the Son of Man has the power to forgive sins"? In other words, if Jesus can't do physical miracles, what reason is there to think that he can do spiritual miracles? After all, spiritual miracles (healing our broken souls and corrupt minds) are a lot more difficult than just multiplying a few loaves of bread. If it weren't for his miracles, we might despair of ever becoming whole.

St. Augustine points out that Jesus brought three people back from the dead (before His own Resurrection): Jairus' daughter, the widow's son, and Lazarus. He then goes on to say that the reason Jesus brought these three back from the dead is so that we might believe that he could heal us from three degrees of sin:

Jairus' daughter has just died; the body's still warm. The widow's son has been dead a bit longer, and the body is actually on the way to the cemetery to be buried. Lazarus, though, is rotted. He's been in the tomb four days, and he stinks. He's so far gone, that if you looked at his corpse at this stage, you probably couldn't even imagine what he looked like alive. And yet, Jesus physically brings all three back to life.

Well, Augustine says those are the three types of sins from which Christ can heal us. There are the sins we just commit one moment and then are sorry for the next—sins that we only give in to briefly, just like Jairus' daughter only gave in to death briefly. Then there are sins that are turning into vices, sins that are taking us on a path to the grave, just like the widow's son was being taken to the grave. And then there are sins and disorders in our soul which are so deep inside us that we can't imagine ourselves without them—just like if we saw Lazarus' corpse we wouldn't imagine what he looked like alive. These are vices and issues that we think it's hopeless to struggle against, that "that's just the way we are." But it doesn't have to be. Jesus took a rotted corpse and turned it back into a healthy, living man. He can take the deepest rot in our souls and make it whole and alive again, and transform us into the persons we were meant to be. That's the hope His miracles should give us.

DIFFERENCE #3:
JESUS SAID HE WAS GOD

Now we come to the most dramatic difference between Jesus and any other religious founder, or really, between Jesus and any other person history has ever taken seriously.

Jesus said He was God. That's right. The thirty-something carpenter's son from a small little town called Nazareth said he was the Eternal Creator of the Universe. He actually said "Before Abraham was, I AM" (thus giving himself the name of the eternal, all-powerful creator of everything). That's one of the things that made the Jews so angry with Jesus: "He made himself God's equal" (John 5;18).

Now what can you do with that? First of all, that's radically unlike what any religious founder would have said. C.S. Lewis imagines what other religious founders would have said if you'd asked them, "Are you the creator of the universe?" Socrates would have laughed at you. Buddha would have urged you to seek enlightenment. Confucius would have said something like, "Jokes which are in bad taste should not be made." And Mohammed would have cut off your head for blasphemy.

I once talked to a nonbeliever who said that Jesus was a good guy, had some good insights, but was a little neurotic. But calling yourself the creator of the universe doesn't qualify you as neurotic: it means you're a full-blown psychotic. If somebody says "I'm the eternal, all-powerful creator of the universe," you don't say, "Well, I disagree with you about that. But I'd still like to hear your views on marriage, family, social justice, and morality in general." Somebody who thinks they're God (with a capital G!) is not someone who's going to give you good moral insights. *But everyone agrees that Jesus had some of the most beautiful moral insights the world has ever known.*

Which means He isn't a psychotic (and remember, thinking you're God isn't the sort of honest mistake a sane person can make). But if He's not psychotic, then when He says that He's God, He must be speaking truthfully. Which means He really is God.

Some people try to lay the blame on the biblical writers. They say, "Oh, Jesus never said He was God. That's just stuff that the Gospel writers put in afterwards." But that won't work either, because the same inconsistency surfaces at the level of the evangelists: on the one hand, you have people who are capable of appreciating and proclaiming love of neighbor, love of enemy, mercy, non-judgmentalism, profound empathy with the poor, condemnation of revenge, etc… and then on the other hand the same people are going around making up the most extravagant, implausible and mischievous lies. That's impossible. The evangelists recorded the beautiful principles of the Gospels because they believed in goodness and truth. That means they weren't the sort of people to go around inventing filthy lies about the man who preached truth and sincerity. So when they record that Jesus said He was God, it's because He really *did* say He was God. There's no other plausible option. And the reason He *said* He was God, was because He really *was* (and *is*) God. There's no other plausible option.

So Jesus is the real deal. You can bet on it. You can bet your life on it. There's no other bet so certain, so assured, so guaranteed to pay off. Because Jesus alone is Lord. There's never been anyone else like Him.

Chapter Five

Reason #4: The Resurrection (Did Jesus Really Rise from the Dead?)

The most celebrated thing that Jesus is said to have done is to Rise from the Dead after three days in the tomb. This fact, the fact that Jesus came back to life—or rather, "walked in newness of life"—was the central teaching of the early Christians. It is the greatest of the miracles of Jesus and the *Catechism* teaches that, "all truths [of the Catholic Faith] even those most inaccessible to human reason, find their justification if Christ by his Resurrection has given the definitive proof of his divine authority, which he had promised," (CCC 651). This is why Saint Paul can say that, "If Christ has not been raised then our preaching is in vain your faith is in vain, (1 Cor 15:14). It is utterly unique to Jesus and this is why again and again the apostles proclaim the good news: Jesus is Risen!

Obviously, most non-Christians reject this claim, and even those who self-identify as Christian may wonder whether there's any evidence to support such a radical position. In this chapter, then, we'll look at the evidence for Christ's Resurrection, and then see why it would actually matter.

Denials of the Resurrection

Everybody accepts that Jesus was a real person, that He lived in the first half of the first century and was put to death by crucifixion. Nobody really argues about this, it's recorded by secular historians as well as by the New Testament, so at least on this basic point Christians and non-Christians agree.

The disagreement, as we saw, concerns the Resurrection. If Jesus didn't really rise from the dead, how did the story that He did get started in the first place? There are about four basic options from a non-Christian perspective:

a) The Resurrection story was made up much later
b) The disciples hallucinated that Jesus had come back from the dead
c) The disciples lied and stole Christ's body to support their lie
d) Jesus faked his own death and then pretended to have come back from the dead

The Resurrection Story Was Made Up Much Later

Some people think that the story of Jesus' Resurrection from the dead was first invented generations after Jesus actually died.

There are many difficulties with that theory, but the main problem is a text from St. Paul's writings to the church of Corinth:

> For I delivered to you first of all what I also received, that Christ died for our sins in accordance with the Scriptures, and that he was buried, and that he was raised on the third day in accordance with the Scriptures and that he appeared to Cephas, then to the Twelve. Then he appeared to more than five hundred brethren at one time, most of whom are still alive, though some have fallen asleep. Then he appeared to James, then to all the apostles. Last of all, as to one untimely born, he appeared to me (I Corinthians 15:3–8).

Now if you want you can deny that St. Paul wrote this passage (although on what grounds?). But clearly whoever's writing this is writing to assure people of the truth of Jesus' Resurrection. And to convince people he cites over five hundred eyewitnesses *most of whom are still alive at the time*. In other words, the author is saying, "Listen, some of the original witnesses are dead, but there are still a lot of people alive right now who saw Jesus risen from the dead." But that claim wouldn't have any force at all if it was written generations after Jesus lived and died—in fact it would be obviously and pathetically impossible. For it to make sense at all that line had to be penned when it was still plausible for someone from Jesus' day to still be living.[2] Therefore, within a lifetime after Jesus people were witnessing to the Resurrection. Which means that the story of the Resurrection wasn't invented generations after Jesus' time; it was part of the preaching of the first generation of Christians.

The Disciples Hallucinated That Jesus Had Come Back from the Dead

Some people say that the apostles were so psychologically wounded by the event of the crucifixion, and that they so desperately wanted to believe that Jesus would rise, that they actually hallucinated and thought they saw Jesus alive, even though actually He was still dead.

Well, the first answer to this suggestion is that the disciples clearly *didn't* want to believe that Jesus would rise. That's why the apostles didn't believe the testimony of the women when they said Jesus had risen, and why Thomas didn't even believe the other apostles. They'd seen Jesus die,

---

2   You could say that someone forged this passage, generations later, in order to pretend that in Paul's time there had been a lot of witnesses to the Resurrection. But then why would the forger bother pointing out that some of his made-up witnesses were dead (i.e., had "fallen asleep")? If you're going to invent a group of witnesses, why on earth would you make some of them dead witnesses? The only answer is that these witnesses weren't invented, they were real. This passage is a sincere statement: the author really did know these people, and he knew that some of them had died.

and they had no expectation that He wasn't just going to stay dead. So you can't really make a case for wish-fulfillment when the people we read about in the Gospel clearly weren't even wishing for Jesus to come back.

Here's the second problem with that suggestion: the Gospels tell us of Jesus appearing to many people at once. Now if these "appearances" are hallucinations, then we have a major dilemma, because as it happens *there is no such thing as a group hallucination*. Hallucinations are like dreams—they are mental events cut off from the external world. But the external world is what unites people's minds, which means if you separate a mental event from the external world you are separating that mental event from other people's minds. Which is why you can't synchronize dreams: you can't get a group of people to dream the same dream at the same time.[3] And for the same reason you can't synchronize hallucinations: you can't get a group of people to have the same hallucination at the same time. So if many people saw Jesus at the same time, that means it wasn't a hallucination.

Now a third problem: Matthew says that the anti-Resurrection story of his day was that the body had been stolen from the tomb. Let's take a look:

> While they were going, behold, some of the guard went into the city and told the chief priests all that had taken place. And when they had assembled with the elders and taken counsel, they gave a sum of money to the soldiers and said, "Tell people, 'His disciples came by night and stole him away while we were asleep.' And if this comes to the governor's ears, we will satisfy him and keep

---

3 You *can* get many people to have the same illusion at the same time, which is what a magician does. But in that case you've got something objective happening in the external world, and the audience simply misinterprets it in a predictable way. In other words, an illusion is based in objective reality, and it involves something actually looking different than it really is. So did Jesus, or the apostles, engineer a fabulous, extravagant illusion? Those are the next two alternatives we'll consider.

you out of trouble." So they took the money and did as they were directed; and this story has been spread among the Jews to this day (Matthew 28:11–15).

So what the people were saying to refute the Resurrection was that the disciples had stolen Jesus' body from the tomb. Which implies that even the deniers of the resurrection admitted that the tomb was empty, that Jesus' body wasn't where it had been buried. But if the disciples had simply been hallucinating then the stolen-body story wouldn't have been necessary. The synagogue leaders who opposed the Christians could have just opened the tomb and pointed to Jesus' body. They could have said, "Look, he's still here. You're crazy." So saying the disciples hallucinated doesn't explain the facts: it doesn't explain what actually happened to the body.

The Disciples Lied and Stole Christ's Body to Support Their Lie

What if the disciples just made the whole thing up? What if the whole story of the Resurrection was a fabrication by the apostles?

Well, there are plenty of problems with this account too. For instance, why would these people intent on spreading Christ's message of love and truth base their whole testimony on a cheap lie? Why would they pretend that women—whose testimony was not well-respected in their culture—had been the first to know that the tomb was empty and Jesus was alive? If they were disappointed by Christ's death ("I guess He's not the Messiah after all"), why didn't they just go back home and try to start over? If they really cared about Jesus enough to dedicate their lives to spreading His story (and many disciples have done just that after the death of their mentor), why wouldn't they just try to spread His story and His teaching without this distracting Resurrection business?

But the main problem with the Deception hypothesis is this: Why would you give your life for a lie? Many of the apostles and first Christians were martyred in horrible, horrible ways. Who on earth would die for something they *know* isn't true? You may give your life for something you *mistakenly think* is true—but we have no case in history of someone dying for something that they know is a hoax. The word "martyr," as is commonly known, is actually taken from the Greek word for "witness," and it is precisely the martyrdom of the early Christians that witnesses to the sincerity of their belief. You may think they were wrong, but they sure didn't think they were.

Jesus Faked His Own Death and Then Pretended to Have Come Back from the Dead

This idea respects the apostles' sincerity, but it does so with a really bizarre explanation. The suggestion here is that Jesus, who was executed according to the official, brutal and absolutely lethal government procedure, survives. This is kind of like suggesting that someone survived being drawn and quartered. But it doesn't stop there: this scenario says that Jesus not only survived crucifixion, he also sneaked out of the tomb (rolling away the huge boulder by himself?), and then appeared to the apostles. How did he appear to them?

Did He appear to them as a bloody, broken mess? If that were the case the apostles would have celebrated the fact that He'd amazingly survived (not resurrected) and then given him some hasty and prolonged medical care.

Did He appear to them looking the way He always looked? But if that was the case then why did people have such a hard time recognizing Him? (Remember Mary Magdalen, the disciples on the road to Emmaus, and the apostles fishing—all of them mistook Jesus for a stranger at first, even when they were talking about Him!). Why was His face so different? What had changed, if He hadn't been raised to a new kind of life?

And obviously if Jesus hadn't really died and risen then He wouldn't have ascended on a cloud several weeks later. In fact He would have died eventually in the normal way, surrounded probably by family and friends. In which case the bogus resurrection wouldn't have made such a big impact on the apostles—after all, Jesus had raised Lazarus from the dead, and even in the Old Testament Elijah brought the widow's son back to life. Those kinds of resurrections weren't as big a deal. Of course, it's nice to be raised from the dead, but if you're going to die again then really it's just a delay of death, not a conquering of it. No, there's no doubt about it, even if Jesus had faked his own death and resurrection—which again, is preposterously implausible—it would not explain why, for the disciples, the Resurrection had changed everything.

So these other options just don't seem to adequately account for the facts. What has given Christianity its impetus? What made it spread throughout the empire like wildfire, despite persecution and even martyrdom?

Well, if you want you can always come up with increasingly improbable scenarios. You can make up weirder and weirder stories, and some people do. You can say that Jesus had an evil twin, or that an earthquake opened up right below Jesus' body and swallowed it into the earth, or that Jesus was an alien and that after his crucifixion he was beamed back up to the mother-ship.

But the fact is that from the beginning the Christians were on fire with belief in Christ's Resurrection. The fact is that they weren't lying, and they weren't the victims of hallucination. And Jesus didn't fake it.

Jesus rose from the dead. He rose from the dead to die no more. Why? So that we could too.

Chapter Six

SOME OBJECTIONS TO CHRISTIANITY

Okay, now let's take a look at some common objections to Christianity.

> Q. I'm not a Christian because, after all, Christianity is just one of many religions.

Non-believers sometimes justify their refusal to follow Christianity based on the plurality of religions. What's interesting is that sometimes they say their non-acceptance of Christianity comes from the *similarities* between religions, and sometimes they say their non-acceptance of Christianity comes from the *differences* between religions.

It's true that all the religions in the world have certain **similarities**. They all involve some kind of worship, some kind of morality, some kind of belief in "higher beings" or "higher forces." Sometimes people who have a strong impression about the similarities of all religions will conclude that they're basically all close enough, that they're all pretty good, and that they're "all true."

But the fact is that it's not possible for all religions to be true for the simple reason that all religions contradict one another. And whenever there's a contradiction, at most one person can be right. If person A says 2+2=3, and person B says 2+2=4, and person C says 2+2=5, we know that at most only one of them can be right. It's not enough just to focus on how close A, B, and C's answers are—the fact is that only B is right. So too, when religion A says Jesus Christ was merely a great prophet, and religion B says Jesus Christ was the creator of the universe, and religion C says Jesus Christ was merely a wonderful person and a fine moral teacher, then at most only one of them can be right. So all religions can't be true at the same time—you have to make a choice to accept one of them or none of them, but you can't accept all of them.

Some people, then, look at all the **disagreements** between religions—disagreements about God or about the afterlife or about moral/social issues—and these people conclude that there's too much disagreement. So all religions must be wrong.

But just because there are many different opinions doesn't mean nobody gets it right. As Chesterton points out, that's like saying, "You know, there are a lot of horses in this race. So I don't think any of them can win." Or to switch the analogy, there may be a lot of religious archers shooting, perhaps, at the same target. That will mean that some of the arrows may get close, but there's only room for one arrow right at the center of the bull's eye, and it's our job to find out which religious arrow that is.

And we've now seen the strong evidence (Jesus' miracles, the prophecies foretelling Him, His claim to be the creator of the universe, and the credibility of His Resurrection) that Christianity is the religion that gets it right.

> Q. I don't believe what the Gospels say about Jesus because after all, the Gospel stories are just ancient myths. The Gospel stories about Jesus aren't any different than the stories about Thor or Prometheus.

This comparison of myth and gospel is often made by folks who haven't spent much time reading the Gospels and/or mythology.

The fact is that when you look at religious myths from other cultures, you don't see stories like those in the Gospels. The Gospels are chock-full of people we know—even apart from the Gospels—really existed (e.g., Caesar Augustus, Pontius Pilate, the Herod family, John the Baptist, Caiaphas, and Jesus himself). That doesn't happen in myth; stories about Hercules or Odysseus or Aeneus or even about Arthur or Beowulf aren't packed with people we know are real. Also in myth supernatural events aren't subjected to doubt by the spectators, whereas in the Gospels the people who see miracles react with misinterpretation, mystification, skepticism, rationalization—in other words, the people in the Gospels, unlike the people in myths, act just the way you and I would react to miracles. And in the Gospels the eye to detail, even details with no apparent moral or doctrinal significance, goes far beyond the crude narratives of mythology. As C.S. Lewis, who taught literature at Oxford and Cambridge, put it:

> Read the dialogues: that with the Samaritan woman at the well, or that which follows the healing of the man born blind. Look at its pictures: Jesus (if I may use the word) doodling with his finger in the dust; the unforgettable "and it was night" (John 13:30). I have been reading poems, romances, vision-literature, legends, myths all my life. I know what they are like. I know that not one of them is like this. Of this text there are only two possible views. Either this is reportage... Or else, some unknown writer in the second century, without known predecessors, or successors, suddenly anticipated the whole technique of modern, novelistic, realistic narrative.[4]

In the story of the woman taken in adultery we are told Christ

---

4   "Fern seed and Elephants" or "Modern Biblical Scholarship."

bent down and scribbled in the dust with His finger. Nothing comes of this. No one has ever based any doctrine on it. The art of *inventing* little irrelevant details to make an imaginary scene more convincing is a purely modern art. Surely the only explanation of this passage is that the thing really happened? The author put it in simply because he had *seen* it.[5]

All of which shows that the gospel stories, whatever they are, aren't myths.

> Q. I don't think God really cares whether you believe in Jesus or not. I think all that matters is whether or not you're a good person.

First off, have you ever really tried being a good person? I mean a *really* good person? Because if you have, if you've really made an effort to be fair and courageous and to think your decisions through carefully, and only to say what should be said, and not to act on cravings or impulses you know are addictive and hurtful, and to really behave as though other people are just as important as you are—if you've ever tried to do that then you know it's incredibly difficult. It's hard even to *know* how to be good, let alone actually *being* good. In fact, one of the best preparations for understanding who Jesus is, and why we need Him as our Savior, is actually, sincerely putting "being a good person" as the number one priority of your life. Because when you make that your main goal, you'll really see how desperately you need help. How desperately you need Him.

But maybe what this objection means is that all that matters is that you be an okay person. An average person. Not a psychopath or a sociopath. Maybe what some people mean by "good person" is just a "pretty

---

5 "What are we to make of Jesus Christ?"

good person." But is that really all that matters? Would anybody really say that the main thing in life is to be mediocre? Because if mediocrity is your priority, if that's what matters to you, then you actually have some very serious problems—you are lost in life, and you badly need to get some direction. You need to ask God for help, and you need to be open to the help He sends you.

Here's another point: either Christianity is true or it isn't. If it's true then the things it says about how to be good are true as well. And if you don't recognize that then you won't know as much about how to be good. In other words, if Christianity is true then it matches up with reality—but in that case your ignoring or rejecting Christianity will set you in opposition to reality. And if you're acting against reality then it doesn't matter whether you're a well-wishing sort of person, you'll actually be doing a lot of harm. So if you really care about being good then you simply can't ignore the special claims of the Gospel of Jesus Christ.

And finally, let's talk about what God cares about. Remember, according to the Scriptures God is our Father who loves us dearly. So He wants to be close to us, the way every good Father wants to be close to His children. Do you think it's "good" to ignore the loving Father who gave you everything? To ignore His Son, to ignore His family? Do you think it would be admirable for a child in a loving family to ignore all his relatives because he was too busy being a "good person"?

Consider this illustration: one thing every schoolteacher notices is the difference in class between the students who have a strong, positive relationship with their parents and the students who don't. All the students may be "good kids," but that parental relationship makes a big difference, a difference in the way the students relate to their peers, to authority figures, to assignments. It makes a big difference even to the students' self-image. It's better to be a good kid with a positive parental relationship.

So too, it's better to be a good person with a positive relationship with God the Father, and that's precisely what Jesus Christ came to offer. You can be a good person and an orphan, but it's a harder life without that core relationship. You can be a good person and a non-believer, but it's a harder life without that core relationship.

> Q. I believe in a Creator of the Universe, but I don't think He gets involved with us, or that He intervenes in human history. So I don't believe in Jesus.

Okay, remember that as we saw in the first two chapters, God isn't just a Creator, He's also the Moral Source, the Standard for what counts as good. He's where Good comes from. He is Good in the maximal sense of the word.

So would a good God—who sees what a mess humanity is in, both as individuals and as groups—would a perfectly good God just leave us to our own devices? It would be a strange Perfect Being who designed the human race, put them in a world full of suffering and wickedness, and then just watched as we struggled down here.

Wouldn't it be more like a good God to offer help?

There's only one account of God coming to offer help, and not only coming to offer help but doing it in a way that respects our freedom to refuse His offer if we want to. That account is the Christian account, and it seems to fit better than any other account with both the world as it is and God as we naturally conceive of Him.

Or try it this way: what do you think is the most important thing there is? It's an interesting question, because the answer to it tells you what you venerate, or even what you adore. In fact, you could define **adoration** as *acknowledging that something is the most important thing there is.* **Idolatry** is when you pick the wrong thing to adore.

So what do you think is the most important thing there is? What's your object of adoration? Is it success? Is it survival? Is it fame? Is it food?

Is it yourself?

Is it love?

Hopefully you're willing to recognize that love is the most important thing there is. But if that's your pick, then you should get in line to adore the God of the New Testament. Because He's the only God of love on the market, the only God anyone ever heard of who embodies pure, perfect, and heroic love. Love is the right answer, and so God Incarnate in Jesus Christ is the right God for you.

Why the Catholic Church?

Chapter Seven

WHY WE NEED THE CATHOLIC CHURCH

Let's start this chapter with a very simple question: Do you think Jesus wants all His followers to be divided? Do you think He wants to have thousands of Christian groups who refuse to pray together, who disagree about what's right and wrong, who argue about what Jesus would really want for families, for societies, for worship services, for individuals?

Did you know there are Eastern Orthodox Christians who won't even pray the Our Father with other denominations, because they don't think other Christians really are children of God? And of course Evangelicals won't pray the Hail Mary with Catholics, because they think it's blasphemous to pray to the Blessed Virgin.

Some Christians think the Eucharist is really Christ's Body and Blood and that we should adore it; others think it's just a symbol and it shouldn't be adored. Some Christians think you need to *do* certain things to be saved; others think you just have to *believe* certain things to be saved.

It should be fairly obvious that this isn't what Jesus would want. In fact, He specifically prayed that His apostles and those who listened to them would be united: "I do not pray for these only, but also for those who believe in me through their word, that they may all be one; even as you Father are in me, and I in you, that they also may be in us, so that the world may believe that you have sent me" (John 17:21–22).

In other words, Jesus is saying that if Christians are united, it will help the world believe that Jesus is really from God. But the implication is that if Christians *aren't* united it will be harder for the world to accept Christ. And it's true. I know an atheist who stands in front of audiences and goes through a list of all the controversial current social issues. Then he says, "And on every single one of these issues, Christians are divided. So what practical difference does Christ make in people's lives?" He's got a point.

This division isn't how Christianity is supposed to be. St. Paul, in his first letter to the Corinthians, says, "I urge you, brothers, in the name of our Lord Jesus Christ, that all of you agree in what you say, and that there be no divisions among you, but that you all be united in the same mind and in the same purpose" (1:10).

So Christians should be undivided in what they say, in what they think, and in what they do. That's a pretty tall order; how do you fill it?

The Bible

For starters the Bible definitely can't unite all Christians. That's why we have all these different Bible-believing denominations. The Bible just isn't enough to make the people who accept it agree with one another.

That's one of the reasons the idea of *Sola Scriptura* (Scripture alone) is such a strange idea—because the Bible obviously can't give Christians one of the main things they need, namely, unity.

There are a couple of other problems with saying that the Bible is "all you need" for being able to know Jesus and to know what it takes to follow Him.

For one thing, it goes against the history of Christianity. How was Christianity first spread? It wasn't by putting Bibles in hotel rooms, or by mass-producing copies of the Gospels. The Bible didn't even exist yet, or at least not the parts of the Bible (the Gospels) that explicitly talk about Jesus. The apostles didn't make their first converts through *writing*, but through *preaching*. Then afterwards a) the apostles and b) those authorized by the apostles, wrote down the life and teachings of Our Lord. So obviously it can't be that the Bible is the only way to know Jesus—because the first Christians came to know Jesus not through the Bible but through the preaching of the apostles.

Which brings us to the second problem with the "Scripture Alone" idea, namely, Where did the Bible come from? As we just saw, it was the apostles who wrote and authorized the parts of the Bible that refer explicitly to Jesus. But then who was it that decided which writings should be included in the Bible and which shouldn't? After all, there were a lot of writings floating around in the early centuries of Christianity—letters from early martyrs like Ignatius of Antioch, Gnostic gospels full of bizarre and fanciful stories about Jesus, apocryphal Jewish writings like the Book of Enoch—so how do we know which books count as biblical, as being revealed by God?

The answer is that it was Pope Damasus at the end of the fourth century who directly determined which books were to be included in the official collection of the Scriptures. He commissioned St. Jerome to make an official translation which contained all the Old and New Testament writings. That official edition of the Bible, called the Vulgate, was then reaffirmed by the Bishops of the world at the Ecumenical Council of Trent in the sixteenth century. To put it briefly, the successor of Peter (the pope) and the successors of the apostles (the bishops) collected the inspired writings into a single volume, which today we call the Bible.

Ask any other set of Christians how we know which books count as Scripture, and their answer will almost always be very vague. But the Catholic answer is clear: the Church wrote and collected the Scriptures. So it doesn't make much sense to accept the Bible but not accept the community that gave us the Bible.

The last problem with saying "You should only believe what's in the Bible" is that nowhere does the Bible itself say that! The Bible doesn't say that the Bible's all you need. Which means that the idea of *Sola Scriptura* is actually self-undermining.

Quite the contrary, the Bible talks about the importance of the Church, and about the bishops (the Greek New Testament word is *episkopos*, cf., Titus 1:7), and about how they have to preserve what's been handed on to them from the apostles (see especially Paul's letters to Timothy, bishop of Ephesus: I Timothy 4:13–16; 6:20; II Timothy 1:13–14).

Again, what's the point? The point is that while we do need the Scriptures (without them we'd basically lose all contact with Christ Jesus), the fact remains that the Bible isn't a stand-alone book. It's a book that comes to us through the hands of the Church and testifies to the Church, such that it only makes sense to believe in the Bible if you believe in the Church too.

So What Does the Church of Jesus Christ Look Like?

The first record we have of the Church of Jesus Christ is the Pentecost event described in the book of Acts, chapter two. Here we have a little group of Jesus' followers who remain together after Jesus ascends to Heaven on a cloud. So far so good: but then the Holy Spirit comes down on the group in fire, and *whoosh*, this group gets busy. Within one day they've upped their membership to three thousand souls, and counting. The rest of the book of Acts is the story of this Church, how Jesus' Church grows and develops during the first generation of Christians. So what does this Church look like?

Well, let's go back to Acts chapter two, to that Pentecost event, which has traditionally been called "The Birth of the Church." This one chapter of the New Testament can tell us an enormous amount about what Jesus' Church looked like from the beginning.

First of all, that first Church had unity: "And all who believed were together and had all things in common" (Acts 2:44). So this Church was able to do precisely what the Bible cannot, namely, unite all believers. We've seen already how important it is that Christ's followers not be divided in what they say, do or think—and by the grace of the Holy Spirit that was able to happen for the members of that first Christian community. The first Church, the Church of Pentecost is **One** Church.

Secondly, this first Church has holiness. It has the Holy Spirit working through it, sanctifying people. More specifically, this Church has sacraments ("sacraments" are derived from the same word as "sacred," meaning "holy"). Anyway, throughout the book of Acts the people who hear and accept the good news of Christ are baptized (Acts 2:41). They're also committed to "the breaking of the bread," (Acts 2:42) which is the New Testament expression for the Eucharist (remember that at the Last Supper, when Jesus instituted the Eucharist He "took bread, blessed it, *and broke it*, and gave it to the disciples and said, "Take, eat; this is my body"—Matthew 26:26). So the first Church lays a lot of emphasis on Baptism and the Eucharist. These sacraments are clearly linked to the Church's status as a **Holy** Church.

Thirdly, this first Church is diverse. It's open to anyone and brings in people from many different backgrounds. The Church's first proclamation of Jesus was to "devout men from every nation under heaven... Parthians and Medes and Elamites and residents of Mesopotamia Judea and Cappadocia, Pontus and Asia, Phrygia and Pamphylia, Egypt and the Parts of Libya belonging to Cyrene, and visitors from Rome, both Jews and proselytes, Cretens and Arabians, we hear them telling in our own tongues the mighty works of God" (Acts 2:5-11). Thus, from its earliest days, the Church is universal—it seeks everyone, from every culture and ethnicity, and it will proclaim the message of Jesus in every language. The Church of Christ is **Catholic**, which is derived from the Greek word *katholikos*, meaning "universal."

Finally, the Church of Pentecost is led and taught by the apostles, "And they devoted themselves to the apostles' teaching" (Acts 2:42). Who originally spreads the message of the Gospel? Peter and the apostles. When the people have a clear question ("What must we do?" from Acts 2:37), of whom do they ask it? Of Peter and the apostles, and it's from them that they get a clear answer. So the early Church is **Apostolic**.

These are the four characteristics displayed at Pentecost at the Church's birth; you might say they're the Church's four birth-marks. In fact, they're officially known as the four "Marks of the Church," the indications for when you know that you've found the faith-community founded by Jesus. And by the way, this wasn't a list Catholics invented recently; this list has been around since the early part of the fourth century. So the million-dollar question is: what Christian church is most obviously One, Holy, Catholic and Apostolic? Or, to put it differently, which church is the most like the Church at Pentecost?

Let's begin with Unity. Which church has the power to unite the most people? Which church can get the most people to pray together, worship together? Easy: the Catholic Church. It's by far the largest denomination of the largest religion in the world. It's huge, it's enormous. And it's growing. It boasts over a billion members, and within a couple decades is expected to grow to a billion and a half. So if you're looking for a Church that does a really good job with unity, look no further.

Now go to Holiness. True, the members of the Catholic Church are often a mess, morally speaking. But look at all the saints! Look at the Padre Pios and Mother Teresas and John Paul IIs. And remember that in Acts the focus of the early Church was the sacraments, especially Baptism and the Eucharist. What church do you know that lays the most emphasis on

Baptism and the Eucharist?

It gets really easy when you come to Catholic. There's only one Catholic Church, and no one else even tries to take the name. Just three hundred years after Our Lord's death and resurrection, St. Cyril would say to new Christians, "If ever you are travelling in any city, do not ask simply where the Lord's house is... nor merely where the Church is, but where is the Catholic Church. For this is the peculiar name of this Holy Body, the Mother of us all, which is the Spouse of our Lord Jesus Christ."[6] St. Augustine (who died in 430 a.d.) says the same thing: "Although all heretics wish to be called Catholics, nevertheless to any stranger who asked where to find the 'Catholic' Church, none of them would dare to point to his own basilica or home."[7]

I recently saw an anti-Catholic book, and on the back cover it warned, "The Catholic Church is the largest international organization in the world." The author had meant to make the Catholic Church look sinister and menacing, but actually he showed that the Catholic Church is the same Church as the Church at Pentecost, which was able to spread the Gospel to "devout men from every nation under heaven." The Church went to all nations and cultures then, and the same Church goes to all nations and cultures now.

Finally, Apostolic. Again, this one is pretty easy. The Church at Pentecost was led by the apostles, with Peter at their center as the spokesman. What church today is led by the successors of the apostles, with the successor of Peter at their center as the spokesman?

It's pretty straightforward, really. Of all the churches today, one Church, the big one, clearly carries the marks of Christ's original Church. The Catholic Church is the faith-community which is one, holy, catholic

---

6   *Cat, xviii,* 26.
7   *Contra Ep. Manich,* 5.

and apostolic.

Saved in Isolation, or Saved in Community?

When God built humanity, He built us for interdependence. We see this on the natural level with the organizations we're all a part of: families, civil societies, schools, corporations, etc... As Aristotle put it, "Man is, by nature, a social animal."[8] It's part of our nature to construct these societies, and each one of these natural societies can be characterized by three features:

1. The members of the society each have different talents and resources.
2. Because of this, there are a variety of roles in the society (i.e., different people are assigned different tasks).
3. If one person fails at his role, it does damage to the rest of the society.

Now that's just on the level of nature; that's just the things we do regardless of whether we're Christian or not. But then God sends Christ, and Christ sends the Spirit to build a Church—that is, a *supernatural society*—on Pentecost. And presumably this supernatural society is going to exhibit some of the same features as the natural societies. After all, there's always some similarity between the way we live as mere creatures and the way we live as Children of God; God tends to maintain a consistent style. So just as He ordained that our earthly life should be in community and interdependence, so too has He ordained our supernatural life.

You can't say, "I can do it on my own" in life. That's not how God designed things. You didn't give birth to yourself, you didn't raise your-

---

8 *Politics*, I, 2.

self, and odds are that even now you couldn't survive by yourself. I know I couldn't—if someone dumped me naked in the woods and said, "Now live the rest of your life without other people" I'd be a goner.

The same goes for living as a disciple of Jesus Christ. You can't just say, "I'll do it on my own," because that's not the way God's set it up. He's made it so we need to live in natural society and so we need to live in supernatural society. We need the Church.

Chapter Eight

The Church as Jesus' Body

Maybe the best way to start this chapter is just to look at a bunch of different misconceptions by which people fail to understand the Church. Here's a list of things you've probably heard somebody say at one time or another:

"I can accept Jesus without accepting the Church."

"The Church gets in the way of my relationship with Jesus."

"I think the Church is just the invisible connection between all believers."

"I believe in Jesus, but I don't believe in organized religion."

And finally, just for good measure: "I don't get why Catholics have a pope."

Now it's not surprising that there are so many objections to the idea of the Church; but what *is* surprising is that in a very real way all of these objections can be addressed by understanding the Church as the Body of Christ.

It's St. Paul who first spoke of the Church as Christ's Body, and he did it on quite a number of occasions (Cf., 1 Corinthians 12:12–31; Colossians 1:18; 2:18–20; Ephesians 1:22–23). It's a fascinating idea, and once you grasp it you see the implications are enormous. Basically, according to this model, if you want to understand the connection between Jesus and the Church, you just have to figure out what a person's connection to his own body is. So how about it? How are you and your body connected? How do we relate to our bodies?

WE IDENTIFY OURSELVES WITH OUR BODIES

The first thing to notice, and it's an incredibly striking thing, is that we talk about our bodies as though they were *ourselves*. Because in a way they are. Think of all the times you're talking about your body, and you substitute "me" or "I":

"How do I look?"

"Look how high I can jump!"

"Pass me the ball."

Obviously, in these cases you're not talking about your soul: you aren't asking how your soul looks, or saying that your soul's a good jumper, or asking someone to pass the ball to your soul. You're talking about your body, and you're *identifying yourself with your body*. We do it all the time. If you play hide and seek with a little kid, and you discover his hiding spot, the kid doesn't say, "You found my body!" He says, "You found me!" And if you were to hit someone for no reason, that person would *not* say, "Well, I'm glad you didn't do anything to me. But, just out of interest, why'd you hit my body?" The person would say, with some justifiable indignation, "Why'd you hit me?!" Because what we do to a person's body, we do to that person.

Now when a man named Saul was persecuting the Church, and the Lord interrupted him by knocking him off his horse, what did Jesus say? Did He say, "Saul, Saul, why are you persecuting my believers, my followers, my community? Why are you persecuting these people?" No. What

Jesus said, and what Saul—who became Paul—remembered for the rest of his life, was, "Saul, Saul, why are you persecuting me?"

In other words, Jesus relates to His Body—the Church—the way we relate to our bodies, namely, *He identifies Himself with His Church*. Which means that what you do to the Church, you do to Christ. Paul was persecuting the Church, which meant He was persecuting Christ. And that goes for all the rest of it too: if we accept the Church, we accept Christ. If we're indifferent to the Church, we're indifferent to Christ. If we reject the Church, we reject Christ.

So what does it not make sense to say? It does not make sense to say, "I can accept Jesus without accepting the Church." Someone who says that is as confused as Saul before he was knocked off his horse.

Our Bodies Are How We Relate to Other People

What connects us to other persons? How do we get to know somebody else? The answer is fairly obvious: *through the body!* The only way I know anybody else is out there is if I see his body with my bodily eyes, hear her bodily voice with my bodily ears. That's the only way we can communicate, through the body: through a spoken or written word, a gesture, a facial expression, a handshake, a hug, etc… Again, the point is that *the human person communicates and enters into a relationship with other persons through the body*. We don't have ESP; we need the body as an interface in order to connect to each other on the personal level.

So if the Church is Christ's Body, then that means Christ communicates and enters into a relationship with us through the Church.

I speak to people through my body. Christ speaks to us through His Church. I express my love for people by smiling, shaking hands, embracing, using my mouth and vocal chords to form loving sentences—in other words, I express my love for people through my body. Christ expresses his love for us through the Church.

Can you imagine if a husband said to his wife, "I want to get to know you better, but your body is kind of in the way." That right there is a husband headed straight for the doghouse.

And yet it's essentially the same thing when believers say, "I want to get to know Christ better, but the Church is kind of in the way." What a failure to understand the Church as Christ's Body! The Church isn't an *impediment* to relationship with Jesus, it is the *vehicle* for relationship with Jesus. It's how He relates to us and how we relate to Him.

So what does it not make sense to say? It does not make sense to say, "The Church gets in the way of my relationship with Jesus."

OUR BODIES ARE OUR PHYSICAL PRESENCE IN THE WORLD

By definition, a body is physical. That's what the word "body" means: an object in the physical world. And when we talk about the human body, we're talking about the physical part of a human being. The part you can see, the part that's accessible to the senses.

So when the New Testament tells us that the Church is the Body of Christ, it means that the Church is the physical, visible presence of Jesus in the world.

God knows we're physical beings, which is why God has always come to humanity in physical, sensory ways. In the Old Testament God came through a burning bush, a pillar of cloud, or small voice you could barely hear. During the thirty-three years when Christ walked the earth, God came through Christ's visible humanity. Now, in this third phase of salvation history, God comes to us through the Church.

God comes to us through the smell of incense, through the sound of the priest's absolution, through the taste of the Eucharist. He comes to us through the feel of the blessed oil on our hands and head as we're preparing to die. And He comes to us through the sight of the basilicas and the stained-glass windows and the paintings and the sculptures—masterworks of beauty made by Michelangelo and Titian and Bernini and hundreds of thousands of artists you never heard of—all dedicated to the glory of God.

All this is the Church, all this is the Church of Christ. This is His Body, His physical presence in the world.

So what does it not make sense to say? It does not make sense to say, "I think the Church is just the invisible connection between all believers."

Our Bodies Are Organisms

Some people have this thing against "organized religion." They seem to think that for some reason if religion is organized it becomes corrupted.

It's hard to know where this idea comes from, but certainly it doesn't come from Our Lord. Jesus is very organized. He even sets up a basic leadership structure to match the surrounding social structure. In Matthew, for instance, he chooses twelve apostles, who of course correspond to the twelve tribes of Israel. In Luke, though, he selects seventy disciples, who correspond to the number of nations enumerated in the book of Genesis (Genesis 10). In any case, it clearly won't work for an admirer of Christ to disparage "organized religion," for Christ founded a community that has a very clear, and very efficient structure.

Besides that, once we grasp that the Church is Christ's Body, then we know that the Church has to be organized, for the simple reason that a person's body is organized. It is, after all, called an "organism," and its component parts are called "organs."

Obviously, the various parts of the body each have set roles and functions, and all have to cooperate for the body as a whole to flourish. Many people seem to think of Christianity as a collection of individual and basically identical units, each doing its own thing. But that's not how a body works. A body isn't made up of identical parts each doing their own thing;

it's made up of very different parts all working together. And, as St. Paul reminds us, what each one does affects the rest. If the hand brings only unhealthy food to the mouth, it's going to hurt the heart—if the heart stops pumping blood, the hand dies.

The Catholic Church has the most sophisticated and successful organizational structure of any corporation on earth. Even atheistic philosophers like Auguste Comte recognized that no other society or institution had ever had such an effective model as the Catholic Church. And no wonder. There's only one institution that God came to earth to establish personally.

So what does it not make sense to say? It does not make sense to say, "I believe in Jesus, but I don't believe in organized religion."

Every Person Uses His Head to Govern His Body

Not to use too violent an image, but if you cut a person's head off, that person will no longer be able to govern his body. You can't tell your hands what to do, or your feet what to do, unless you have a head with which to tell them.

So if the Church is Christ's Body, what is the head that Christ uses to govern this body?

Some people will tell you that Christ Himself is the head. And that's true, of course, if we mean simply that Christ rules over the Church, or that Christ is in charge of the Church.

But *how* does Christ rule over the Church? After all, we can't see Christ anymore. So, to us, Christ is no longer a visible head of the Church.

Now many Protestant Christians will say that the Church is invisible—the invisible connection between believers—and so it's fine for the Head of the Church to be invisible as well. But as we saw a moment ago, that doesn't work. The Church is a body, it's something physical, and it's something visible. And so the head of the body should be physical and visible too.

Many Eastern Orthodox Christians will acknowledge that the Church is physical and visible, but then they'll say that Christ rules the Church invisibly. But that's basically like saying that you have a physical body that's missing its physical head—and that obviously doesn't work.

So what we need is a Church with a definite, visible structure, and a definite, visible source of leadership. Which is why Christ gave His Church a Pope.

Jesus Instituted the Papacy

There are a number of places in the New Testament where we can see Jesus making Peter the head of the Church. The most famous passage in this context is Matthew 16:13–20:

> When Jesus went into the region of Caesarea Philippi he asked his disciples, "Who do people say that the Son of Man is?" They replied, "Some say John the Baptist, others Elijah, still others Jeremiah or one of the prophets." He said to them, "But who do you say that I am?" Simon Peter said in reply, "You are the Messiah, the Son of the living God." Jesus said to him in reply, "Blessed are you, Simon son of Jonah. For flesh and blood has not revealed this to you, but my heavenly Father. And so I say to you, you are Peter, and upon this rock I will build my church, and the jaws of death shall not prevail against it. I will give you the keys to the kingdom of heaven. Whatever you bind on earth shall be bound in heaven; and whatever you loose on earth shall be loosed in heaven."

It's very common in Catholic circles to compare this passage with an Old Testament passage where God chooses Eliakim as the kingdom's prime minister:

> On that day I will summon my servant Eliakim, son of Hilkiah; I will clothe him with your robe, gird him with your sash, confer on him your authority. He shall be a father to the inhabitants of Jerusalem, and to the house of Judah. I will place the key of the House of David on his shoulder; what he opens, no one will shut, what he shuts, no one will open. I will fix him as a peg in a firm place, seat of honor for his ancestral house; On him shall hang all the glory of his ancestral house: descendants and offspring, all the little dishes, from bowls to jugs. On that day, says the LORD of hosts, the peg fixed in a firm place shall give way, break off and fall, and the weight that hung on it shall be done away with; for the LORD has spoken (Isaiah 22:20–25).

There are quite a few correspondences between these two passages, including the following: a) Eliakim gets the keys to the house of David, Peter gets the keys to the kingdom of Heaven; b) What Eliakim opens no one shall shut, what Peter binds on earth will be bound in Heaven (in other words, there is a permanence to their decisions—one cannot appeal their decisions to some higher authority); c) Eliakim is a "peg in a secure place" upon which everything hangs; Peter is the rock upon which the Church is built. So Peter and Eliakim are the secure points of their communities. If a peg falls, everything hanging on it falls as well and smashes into a lot of little pieces. And, as Our Lord says elsewhere, if you build your house on something other than rock, the whole house falls to pieces. This is precisely what we see with those Christians who do not accept the office of Peter—namely, the papacy. These communities are in a constant state of division, so that we have a great multitude of denominations, and it's because they don't have a foundation strong enough to preserve unity.

These correspondences between Eliakim and Peter make it clear that both are being instituted as the prime ministers of God's kingdom. But there's one difference: Isaiah says that one day the peg that is Eliakim will give way, and everything that depends on him will be smashed. So Eliakim's prime ministry is temporary. On the contrary, the rock that is Peter will never be destroyed; "the jaws of death" will not prevail against it. Which is why even though the prime ministry of the davidic kingdom of Israel has long since passed out of memory, Peter's office, the line of popes, has continued down to the present day.

By the way, sometimes other Christians will claim that Jesus wasn't calling *Peter* the rock of the Church, but was rather calling *acknowledgement of Christ as the Son of God* the rock of the Church. This is a weird and, honestly, a fairly tortured interpretation of the passage. Jesus gives Simon a new name, and explicitly connects this name to being the foundation stone of the Church. He says "You are Rock ("*Petros*," the masculine name-form of "rock") and on this rock ("*petra*," the feminine noun-form of "rock") I will build my Church, and the jaws of death will not prevail against it. I will give to you the keys of the kingdom of heaven, whatever you bind on earth shall be bound in heaven, and whatever you loose on earth shall be loosed in heaven." Now no one denies that at the beginning of the speech, Jesus is talking about Peter. And no one denies that at the end of this speech, Jesus is talking about Peter. But non-Catholics try to say that in the middle of this speech, Jesus is talking about something *completely different* (i.e., a profession of faith in Christ)! But what would give that impression? Jesus literally says, "You are Rock, and on this rock I will build my Church." What possible indication is there that He's talking about two different rocks? No—it may be uncomfortable for people to admit, but there's no getting out of it: Jesus says that Peter is the foundation-stone of the Church.

There are other passages too where Peter is acknowledged in the New

Testament as the Chief Apostle. For instance, in Luke 22: 28–32 Our Lord gives Peter the exclusive mission of strengthening the other apostles. In Matthew 17: 24, 27 Christ instructs Peter to pay tax for the both of them together. Peter thus becomes the public representative of Christ—their identities have become linked, and so too Peter's authority must be respected as Christ's authority.

But two very interesting passages having to do with Peter are found in Luke 12 and John 21. See if you notice the implications of putting these two stories together:

> "But know this, that if the householder had known at what hour the thief was coming, he would have been awake and would not have left his house to be broken into. You also must be ready; for the Son of man is coming at an hour you do not expect." Then Peter said, "Lord, is this parable meant for us or for everyone?" And the Lord replied, "Who then is the faithful and prudent steward whom the master will put in charge of his servants to distribute the food allowance at the proper time?" (Luke 12:41–42).

> "Simon, son of John, do you love me?" He said to him, "Yes, Lord, you know that I love you." He said to him, "Feed my lambs." He then said to him a second time, "Simon, son of John, do you love me?" He said to him, "Yes, Lord, you know that I love you." He said to him, "Tend my sheep." He said to him a third time, "Simon, son of John, do you love me?" Peter was distressed that he had said to him a third time, "Do you love me?" and he said to him, "Lord, you know everything, you know that I love you." Jesus said to him, "Feed my sheep" (John 21:15–18).

So what happens? Well, in the first story Jesus tells Peter that there's going to be one steward whom the master puts in charge of the other servants. Got that? Jesus says there's going to be a steward who's put in charge of the other servants. What is this steward's job description? To "feed" the servants.

So who is the one person that Jesus explicitly instructs to "feed" His followers, His servants, His lambs, His sheep? Surprise, surprise: it's Peter. Which means that Peter is the servant who's been put in charge, by the Master, of the other servants. This is the way God runs his household, by putting one servant in charge of the others. And his household still has a steward, a steward who can trace his lineage back to that first steward, that first rock, the Apostle Peter.

Why Did Jesus Institute the Papacy?

So this is how Jesus set up his Church, with one person in charge. This shouldn't be too surprising. After all, Jesus didn't go around preaching "the democracy of God," or "the aristocracy of God." He went around preaching "the kingdom of God." So which Church today looks most like a kingdom?

But what's the benefit of having a Pope? Well, first of all the pope enables us to **know God's truth**. Throughout the Scriptures, God always sent *prophets* who would proclaim God's truth reliably and without error. And He hasn't stopped sending prophets who proclaim God's truth reliably and without error. They are the popes. That's what Catholics mean by **papal infallibility**: *when the Pope, as successor of Peter, settles something once and for all about faith and morals for the Universal Church, he is preserved from error by God Himself.*

Remember what Jesus said to Peter: "Flesh and blood has not revealed this to you, Simon son of John, but my Father who is in Heaven… What you bind on earth will be bound in Heaven. What you loose on earth will be loosed in Heaven." Simon gets the right answer, not because of his human character (his "flesh and blood"), but by God's grace. So too, the Pope will get the right answer to questions about Christ, not because he's a better human, but because God will keep him safe from error. There have been bad popes and mediocre popes and saintly popes (just as Peter was sometimes bad, sometimes mediocre, and sometimes saintly), but none of the popes have ever officially contradicted one another about the faith. Because we need to know the truth about Christ, and we need to know that it's the truth. Which is why God does not leave His people without a prophet, however unworthy that prophet may be.

The second reason for having a pope is to make it possible for believers to **preserve unity**. As long as everyone in the organization accepts that there's one person in charge, that organization remains *just one organization*. As long as Christians recognize the pope's authority, they remain just one faith community (as we saw in the last chapter, that's not true of the Bible). Historically, whenever a group of Christians reject the pope's authority, it causes a split in Christianity. Sometimes it even causes a chain reaction of splits in Christianity, as in the case of the Reformation. Meanwhile, the Catholic Church remains the largest united group of Christians on earth. The reason is simple: we have one head, and so we are one body.

Chapter Nine

Scandal in the Church

One of the most common complaints against the Church is something to the effect that there are bad Catholics. Something like, "Why would you be a part of an organization that's full of bad people and even bad leaders?"

Well, let's start by admitting that from the very initiation of the Church down to the present day there has been no shortage of those who profess the Catholic faith and have acted in shockingly evil ways. We may think of Judas, our Lord's chosen apostle, or of Alexander VI, perhaps the most infamous of all the popes. Or, more probably, we will think of the recent and horrific scandal of those priests who have been guilty of abusing children. In all of these cases, not only ordinary Catholics, but Catholics in esteemed positions have egregiously violated basic fundamental norms of goodness, decency, and their very humanity. We're not just talking about acts of weakness, but sometimes acts which reach a high intensity of evil.

So how can we make sense of this kind of wickedness with the Church? We say the Church of Christ is holy, but then we see the vile wickedness which is so often associated with her. How can we reconcile these two facts?

The Phenomenon of Scandalmongers

Before proceeding, we need to note that there are definitely people who make it their personal passion to blow the fact of wicked Catholics completely out of proportion. There is commonly a shameless lack of perspective by contemporary culture in recording such scandal; they delight—absolutely *delight*—in finding cases of important Catholics, especially in the hierarchy, especially in the papacy, who have fallen low.

Fulton Sheen discusses this distortion of the papacy:

> The wickedness of one man in authority is allowed to obscure a million saints. But why not get things into proportion? How many who dwell on the Papacy for thirty years during the Renaissance ever dwell on the history of the Papacy for the other hundreds and hundreds of years? How many of those who exploit the bad few ever admit that of the first thirty-three successors of Peter, thirty were martyrs for their faith and the other three exiled for it? How many of those who dwell on the bad example of a few will know or ever admit that of the two hundred and sixty-three successors of St. Peter eighty-three have been canonized for their heroic virtue, and that over fifty were chosen over the protest of their own unworthiness for such a high office? How many who know of the few stains ever mention the courage of a Gregory VII or the great line of saintly and learned men since the Council of Trent, or the saintliness of a Pius IX, the learning of a Leo XIII, the faith of a Pius X, the peace efforts of a Benedict XV, or the saintly wisdom and prudence of a gloriously reigning Pius XI? Anyone who attacks such a long line of martyrs, saints and scholars must be certain of his own sinlessness to lay his hand on the few who revealed the human side of their office. If they are holy, pure and undefiled, let them pick up

their stones.[9]

Obviously, the same could be said with regard to the priest scandals. Why isn't there more mention of all the saintly, awe-inspiring men who give their life away for a supernatural ideal and fight every day to maintain their celibacy?

This brings up a related question: Why do people find Catholic scandal so fascinating? Again, to quote Sheen,

> Why is it that the world is always so scandalized at a scandal in the Church? Why does it always blame a bad Catholic more... if it is not because it expects so much more of the Catholic? Any fallen-away Catholic whose name is quoted as a by-word of sin, and who is supposed to be an argument against the Church, is really a strong Catholic credential... nowhere does evil become so visible as when contrasted with the ideal. The very horror the world expresses at the fall of a Catholic is the measure of the high virtue it expected of him.[10]

If popes, bishops, priests, Catholics are universally recognized as being as sinful as everybody else, why do we take special notice of their sinfulness? It's almost as though the truth and holiness of the Church *is* recognized even in the midst of the sinners associated with Her. It's like people see the contrast between the holiness of the Church and the sinfulness of Her members.

---

9   Fulton Sheen, *The Mystical Body of Christ* (New York: Sheed and Ward, 1935), 151–52.
10 Ibid., 156–57.

How is the Church Perfect, How is the Church Sinful?

One helpful way of making sense of Church scandal and Church holiness is to distinguish between two dimensions of the Church.

The first dimension is the spotless dimension. This dimension includes everything involving the Church's **establishment**, and in this dimension She is perfect.

> Certainly the loving Mother [the Church] is spotless in the sacraments by which she gives birth to and nourishes her children; in the faith which she has always preserved inviolate; in her sacred laws imposed on all; in the evangelical counsels which she recommends; in those heavenly gifts and extraordinary grace through which with inexhaustible fecundity, she generates hosts of martyrs, virgins and confessors.[11]

So, in a) the sacraments, b) the faith, c) the Church's moral vision, d) the "juridical constitution" (i.e., the hierarchical structure), e) the heroism of the saints, f) the gifts of grace. In all these respects you can't find any flaw in the Church. She's perfect, just the way the Lord made Her.

But in all things having to do with **human initiative**, she can be very imperfect:

> And if at times there appears in the Church something that indicates the weakness of our human nature, it should not be attributed to her juridical constitution, but rather to that regrettable inclination to evil found in each individual, which its Divine Founder permits even at times in the most exalted mem-

---

11   Pius XII, *Mystici Corporis*, #66.

bers of His Mystical Body, for the purpose of testing the virtue of the Shepherds no less than of the flocks, and that all may increase the merit of their Christian faith.[12]

So the members of the Church, ("even at times in the most exalted") are imperfect. The same is true for the Church's practical activity, efficiency, self-presentation. All this depends on imperfect human beings, and so we can't expect the Church to be an ideal industrial complex or public relations company. In all these areas God requires human cooperation, and because that cooperation is often withheld through sin and weakness, the Church is riddled with deformity, bureaucracy, ignorance, and vice.

Again, *what the Church officially teaches* and *the way the Church is set up* are divine, holy, and perfect. But those working within the Church are not perfect, they are imperfect and sometimes wicked.

The point, though, is that the sins of its members have zero bearing on the divine perfection of the Church. You can't always blame the organization for the conduct of its members. Take for instance some non-profit thrift store that has a praiseworthy goal, namely, to help the community and make enough earnings to sustain itself. It also has a pretty efficient setup. Let's say the company has been successful, so we can presume it has a working business model. In other words, *both* the **mission** and the **structure** of the company are good, and this combination leads to success. But suppose one day an employee comes to work with a gun and goes on a shooting rampage. Do you think the company would be blamed simply because the murderer was in the store wearing a uniform? Of course not! As a company the store had nothing to do with it. It is in no way part of company policy or company structure to shoot customers—the "employee"

---

12 Ibid.

was actually doing the opposite of what the company guidelines stated, (e.g., "be friendly," etc...).

So too, when a Catholic does evil, it ought not to reflect badly on the Church—the Catholic may be "wearing the uniform" but he's actually diametrically opposed to everything the Church stands for. Judas doesn't negate the goodness of the Apostles or the Truth of Christ, and neither do bad popes, priests or laypeople.

The principle is pretty straightforward: *The Church is holy though her members are sinful.* But then someone might ask, "Well, what's the point of belonging to a holy organization if it doesn't make you holy?"

A good analogy here might be a fitness club. Obviously a health club exists to make people healthy and fit, and it's a great organization to join if you're serious about getting in shape. But it's not enough just to get a gym membership; you also have to go there and follow the program if you want to see any results.

The same thing is true with the Church. It's a great organization to join if you're serious about getting holy—but it's not enough just to join, you also have to follow the Catholic program of truth and virtue and love. If you don't, and bad things happen, then the institution shouldn't be blamed.

Responding to Catholic Scandal

It should be clear, then, that when a Catholic sins, we can just say, "Well, that's a bad Catholic, he doesn't really reflect what Catholicism is." That's a good, safe answer to the problem of Catholic Scandal.

But it also needs to be said that we shouldn't be too quick to believe every Catholic scandal we hear. Sometimes we're comfortable condemning other Catholics with the same enthusiasm as the secular world does. But remember, we're in a family, and in a family you don't just accept an accusation of another family member as soon as you hear it. You look deeper, make sure it's true before you pull out the standard "bad Catholic" defense. You don't just turn your back on a fellow Catholic because they suddenly become very unpopular.

Nonetheless, if a scandal does turn out to be based on true events, how should we respond? Well, firstly with *regret and prayer for the one who is scandalized **and** for the one who is the cause of the scandal*. Remember, we have to love not only victims but perpetrators; Jesus calls us to love not only the innocent, but the guilty.

Secondly, we should respond with *alarm for the good of the Church*. Scandal can hurt the Church more than just about anything else. A traitor hurts a country more than an outside aggressor, and a Catholic can do more damage than a non-Catholic. A shooting inside a store will hurt sales—it's not rational, but if people associate the store with a shooting, they're not going to want to shop there.

Finally, we should have *consolation that the Church doesn't just welcome saints*. Sometimes people may ask, "How could you belong to a group with such awful people, such hypocrites, such dysfunctional individuals?" A good answer to that is, "Well, because I'm dysfunctional, I don't do what I should, I don't live up to the values I preach. I'm a sinner, whose sins brought about the death of the Son of God on a cross. This is exactly where I belong."

Can you imagine if everyone in the Church was a saint, except for you? Lucky for you, the Church is a hospital for sinners, and you should have no trouble fitting in.

Conclusion

THE BASICS OF PRAYER

When I was in grad-school one of my theology teachers told us the story of the man who was so exhausted after finally proving God's existence that he was too tired to pray.

That can happen with apologetics and evangelization too. People spend all their time talking *about* God and never *to* God. It's absurd, unnecessary, and pathetic, like a gourmet chef who enjoys cooking elaborate meals but ends up starving to death because he won't eat anything.

The whole point of *knowing* about God is to *be with* God. God's not interested in being one more item in our worldview; He wants to be Our Father. He wants to know us and have us know Him.

Besides that, our efforts at apologetics or evangelization aren't going to be fruitful unless we're praying. As we saw at the very beginning of this book, no one can convince someone that our faith is true through argument; only the Holy Spirit can really convince someone about Christ and His Church. As St. Paul said, "No one can say that Jesus is Lord except by the Holy Spirit" (I Corinthians 12:3). In other words, we won't be able to bring someone to Jesus if we're just informed. The Spirit also has to be at work in us. We have to be inspired.

If God is going to use us, if we're going to be effective tools in God's hands, we're going to have to get on the same wavelength as He is. That means prayer.

Why We Don't Pray

The main reason people give for not praying is **"I'm too busy."** That's a shocking excuse to use. "I'm to busy to see the Creator of the universe. My to-do list is so important that God Himself can't even get on it." This excuse isn't really an excuse; it's an admission of pride. What we're saying is that what we've got going on is SO important that we can't squeeze God in. Can you imagine saying that to God face-to-face? Think of how you spent your day yesterday, think of everything you did, everything you spent time on. Would you be able to tell God, face-to-face, that every item on that list was more important than talking to Him?

Even God Himself, when He came to earth, found time to pray. Jesus was constantly going off to be by Himself so He could pray. He wouldn't allow anything to distract Him from it; he would leave crowds of sick people, or people who wanted to hear Him talk. God only walked this earth for about thirty-three years; that's not much time to show the divine love, preach the divine truth, heal the sick, save the world!—and yet He constantly found time to pray. God forbid any of us dare say that our work is more important than Christ's. In which case we can take a break from whatever we have going on, and talk to Our Father.

The fact is that our to-do list isn't really so important, and prayer helps us realize that. One of the most immediate effects of prayer is that it chills us out, gives us peace. Talking to God, we realize, "You know what? It'll be okay. I shouldn't be so nerve-wracked about getting it all done. Somehow, the planets will still probably revolve around the sun even if I don't check off everything on my list, or if I don't get every assignment finished as soon as I'd like. Because, after all, I'm not God. You are. You're the One who makes it all happen."

A more honest excuse is **"I don't like to pray"** or **"I feel like I don't get anything out of prayer."** And the proper response to this is: Well, who says prayer has to be all about you? Can you imagine a father who said, "You know, I don't enjoy spending time with my kids. It's not much fun for me; I'd rather be out at a bar or something. Frankly, I don't get a lot out of my children's company. So I think I just won't hang out with them anymore." We would all say shame on that father. Why? Because he's being totally selfish, as though his relationship with his kids is all about him. And we do the same when we act as though prayer has to be all about us.

Hasn't God already done quite a lot for us? Let's see: existence, intelligence, freedom, whatever health we have, whatever education we have, whatever family we have, not to mention salvation through the torture of the cross. So God's already contributed kind of a lot to this relationship. Maybe we should step it up and give a little back, even if we don't feel like it. If we even care a little about this relationship, we shouldn't always be saying to God, "Well, what do I get out of it?" We should be saying, "You've done so much for me. Is there something I can do for You?" And what we can do for Him is pray.

Also, you *will* get something out of prayer, even if you don't notice. I have young kids right now, which means they're growing all the time. But the funny thing is, they don't notice that they're getting bigger and I don't notice they're getting bigger. But when we see friends or relatives whom we haven't seen for a long time they always tell my kids, "Wow, you're growing so fast. You've really shot up; I hardly recognize you."

The same thing happens with prayer: if you spend time with God, He *will* make you grow. You may not notice it, and the people around you may not notice it. But it'll happen. You can't put yourself in God's presence and not be affected. It's going to make a difference.

So pray—pray for God's sake and secondly pray for your sake. Pray out of love for Him and out of a desire for your own happiness.

Finally, people will say, **"I don't know how to pray."** That's a very understandable concern; just sitting in silence with no direction for one's thoughts can be intimidating. The main thing to remember about "how to pray" is that it's a gift of time to God. In other words, when you're praying, *Don't Multitask!* Or at least if you *do* multitask while you pray, don't count that as your daily time with God. It's fine if you want to do some praying in the car, or the shower, or while you're getting some cleaning done, or when you're at your desk and doing something else—but make sure you get some solid time in that's just for God. Make your gift of time a pure gift. It'll mean more to God and will have more rewards for you.

Now there's no one right way to pray, and as with everything else practice makes perfect. However, classical Catholic spirituality does tend to distinguish three basic categories of prayer, which we'll look at right now.

The Three Categories of Prayer

The first basic form of prayer is **vocal prayer**, *the prayers we say out loud*. Vocal prayer is the elementary way in which humans relate to their Maker. Christ Himself encouraged us to pray vocally in teaching us the words of the Our Father.

Vocal prayers can then be divided in four sub-groups: *praise* (acknowledging the goodness and awesomeness of God), *repentance* (expressing sorrow for our sins), *petition* (asking God for things) and *thanksgiving* (expressing our appreciation for the good things God's done for us).

Let's pause and talk very briefly about petition. God wants us to make requests of Him; Jesus Himself encourages us to petition God, to ask Him for the things we want and need. And remember, our petitions do have real consequences. God has made this world such that one event will sometimes cause another event; one domino falling will sometimes cause another domino to fall, and a prayer of petition will sometimes cause the desired result to happen. But that doesn't mean that a petitionary prayer will *always* cause the desired result to happen. Maybe God has something better in mind for us than what we're asking for. Even Jesus, when He prayed for God to "let this cup pass," didn't get what He asked for. So when we pray for something, it should go something like this: "Dear Lord, there's something I want. Maybe the reason I don't have it is because you've already decided that it isn't right for me. And I accept Your will, whatever it is. But just in case You're waiting for me to ask, let me make it official: I'm asking."

Another thing to remember about vocal prayer is that we have to be sure we're not spending *all* our time asking for things. Again, don't make prayer all about you. Often times our prayers include the following phrases: "Give **me** this," "Help **me** with this," "Here's what's happening in **my** life," "What should **I** do?" etc... These sorts of prayers are good, necessary, and not to be disparaged. God wants us to tell Him what we need, and what's going on with us. However there should also be prayers which are focused on God, prayers like: "Thank **You**," "**You** are so good," "**You** have done so much for me," and so on.

The Catholic Church is very rich in vocal prayers: the Rosary, the Chaplet of Mercy, the Stations of the Cross, the Liturgy of the Hours. One of the most powerful vocal prayers is simply to say Our Lord's Name, "Jesus," over and over. Christ's name has enormous power, it brings us to Him and Him to us when we say it with devotion. The Jesus Prayer, which repeats over and over again, "Lord Jesus Christ, Son of God, have mercy on me, a sinner," is an ancient and beautiful way of getting closer to God.

Vocal prayer is always an important part of the spiritual life of every Christian, and we all have to make sure we integrate it into our daily structure.

Nonetheless, we can't stop at vocal prayer. Vocal prayer has to be complemented by **meditation**, or *mental prayer*, a consideration of holy things. Again, there are many ways to meditate, but perhaps the most popular format follows the three-step process of *Read, Reflect, Resolve*.

To begin with place oneself formally in God's presence. Pray to the Holy Spirit for help, ask for His guidance and a receptivity to all his inspirations.

Then *read* something. You can use a book designed for meditation. The Bible is the best book; if you want to hear what God's saying to you, what better way to go about it then to look at the one Book God's actually written? There are a great many other texts as well which are very popular for meditation.[13] But the important thing isn't what you read, it's how you read. Normal reading is done for study, for analysis; it is a task to be finished. You go through the pages and grasp what the author is saying and then you're done. Meditational reading, by contrast, isn't just trying to get through the pages, or to solve some problem with the text. Meditation is a slow savoring.

Which brings us to the second step: *reflect*. What you're trying to do with meditation is allow the Holy Spirit to direct your thoughts. Fulton Sheen describes meditation as riding a horse and holding the reins loosely. You really want to let your horse lead you—so keep a loose hold on your thoughts, and perhaps the Holy Spirit will lead you somewhere. When a thought strikes you or jumps out at you, don't move on with the reading. Instead take that thought as a prompting that God wants you to spend some time with it. Talk to Our Lord about this newfound insight, and ask Him what He wants you to draw from it. Of course, sometimes your thoughts can get out of control; like a horse with the reins loose, your mind might wander way off track. But then you just steer the horse back

---

13   Some examples are, *Imitation of Christ, Divine Intimacy, In Conversation with God, The Way, Furrow, The Life of Christ* by Fulton Sheen.

to the path by returning to your reading. That way the reading acts like an anchor that makes sure you don't drift too far off course.

The third step in meditation is making a *resolution*; this is where you think of some practical application of what you've been thinking about. What do you think God wants you to know, think about, dwell on, do, or integrate into your life? The resolution can be of varying degrees of intensity. It could be something to just keep in mind for the day, or it could be the realization that God wants you to adopt a new behavior for the rest of your life—or anything in between. Finally, before concluding meditation, one should offer a prayer of thanksgiving to God for the opportunity to spend some time with Him, and ask Him for help in carrying out your resolution.

There's a third category of prayer too, which we ought to mention. This is called **contemplation**. In this form of prayer, God takes over. Meditative prayer may involve reading, thinking, imagining, drawing conclusions, and internal effort and focus. Contemplation involves none of these things. In meditation, God is certainly active and guiding our prayer, but we are still basically in control, whereas in contemplation, we are swept up and follow where God leads. Therefore, since contemplation is something initiated and directed by God, it's not an experience we can achieve simply through our own effort and technique. The Lord brings the soul to contemplation when He decides the time is right. In the meantime, we should prepare ourselves by daily fidelity to prayer, identifying and getting rid of mortal and venial sin, by living the gospel with heroic generosity.

Contemplation is the height of human excellence, but God will only grant it to us when we are ready, that is when we are sufficiently purified of sin, when we are constantly self-giving in the ordinary details of life, and when we are faithful to daily prayer.

A Few Final Tips

A critical strategy for getting one's prayer life on track is to plan it out in advance. For instance, we have to plan out what time we'll pray. It's not enough just to say, "I'll pray sometime tomorrow." That's way too general. By the time tomorrow begins, you'll have a ton of stuff to do, there will be unexpected things turning up, someone will want to talk, or you'll get an invitation somewhere, and then when you get home you'll remember all the other stuff you forgot to do, and soon it will be night, and you'll be so tired, and you'll have to get to bed, because you have to get up early, and before you fall asleep, you'll say to yourself, "I'll pray tomorrow." Don't fall into this pattern. Settle on a very specific time beforehand and then plan the rest of the day around it in order to be sure you get your prayer time in.

Secondly, pick a place that's suited to prayerfulness, that is, somewhere with solitude and silence. If I really want to talk to someone about personal stuff, I'm not going to take that person to a bar where we have to scream in each other's ears over the music and ruckus; I'll take him somewhere where we can be alone and undistracted. The same should be true for our time of intimacy with God. It has to be a quiet place, which is one of the reasons that a chapel is such an ideal place to pray. Unfortunately, in our culture it's very difficult to foster silence. We're so used to entertainment and noise that we don't know how to react when we have nothing to do but quietly sit and think. Nonetheless, Jesus tells us to pray in these conditions, "When you pray, go to your inner room, close the door, and pray to your Father in secret" (Matthew 6:6). We must be sure to "shut the door" to keep out all distractions.

Now prayer is a conversation with God; by words, either mental or vocal, we speak to God. Of course when we speak to another person, it's only right that we give him our attention as well as our words, so when we pray the Our Father, or the Hail Mary, or sit in silence, our mind should at least try to be fixed on God or some aspect of our faith/spiritual life. We always expect God to be listening when we talk; let's really try to pay attention when He talks.

Of course everybody struggles with distraction in prayer. Sometimes our thoughts go all over the place, anywhere but God, in fact. That's okay, just keep trying to refocus on the Lord. Practice makes perfect. Also, when you're particularly distracted by one thing in particular, just bring that to Christ. Say, "Lord, as You can tell, I can't stop thinking about this. Can You please help me see why I'm so attached to this? Can You please help me put it in perspective? Can You please use this distraction to bring me closer to You, instead of letting it get in the way?"

Because that's what prayer is. Prayer is the time to come to Christ, to present ourselves and those we love to Jesus. Prayer is our time to give to Our Lord, and allow Him to give to us. Nothing, *nothing*, in life is more important.

Don't make the mistake of learning or talking about Jesus, without going to Him every day. Pray regularly, and let Him equip you to spread the Gospel the way He really wants to.

Oh, and by the way, if you're someone who's gone through this book and *still* doesn't believe in God, or in Christ, or in the Catholic Church, then that just proves my point. I can't convince you. But God can, if you'll really open yourself. If you'll really ask Him to show you that He's real, and that He's sent His Son, and that He wants you to be a member of His universal family. If you ask Him, if you really pray and ask Him, if you sincerely say, "God, if You're real, I do truly want to believe in You and believe in what You've done. So if You're real, please show me." If you say that, He will show you.

Appendix

How Do You Know You Have a Soul?

Why can't the human person be reduced to the merely physical? How do we know we have a soul? Well, we know we have a soul because of two facts:

Fact 1: Persons have immaterial experiences.
Fact 2: Persons perform immaterial actions.

People feel things and do things that just can't be reduced to their biology. And I'm not talking about the occasional mystic or psychic or shaman. I'm talking about you and me and just about everybody else.

People Have Immaterial Experiences

A term often used for inner experiences is **qualia**, and reflecting on them tells us we have to be something more than a body. Over recent decades, philosophers have come up with a lot of ways to prove this point, but one argument has been especially popular:

The Zombie Argument. I bet you thought philosophers were a bunch of boring, old, white dudes with no interest in the living dead. Turns out they like to talk about zombies as much as the next guy. Anyway, imagine planet Earth looking exactly as it does now—all the same forests and oceans and cities and human beings, and the humans have the same biology as real humans, and they say and do exactly what we say and do. The only difference is that folks on the imaginary Earth don't feel anything, or think about anything, or enjoy anything.[14] They walk around and live their lives like organic robots, or zombies.

Can you imagine a world like that? It's kind of creepy, but the fact is you probably *can* see how such a planet would be possible. These zombie-humans are conceivable. They could theoretically exist, although fortunately, they don't exist. How do we know they don't exist? Because we realize that actual human persons *do* have experiences, thoughts and feelings.[15] So we have more than the hypothetical zombies, even though our biology is the same. But that means we're more than our biology. We've got something spiritual going on.

All this just proves, I think, what we already intuitively know. We all have a basic, instinctive sense that we are not just our bodies. I like how the novelist Milan Kundera puts it:

> A long time ago, man would listen in amazement to the sound of regular beats in his chest, never suspecting what they were. He was unable to identify himself with so alien and unfamiliar an object as the body. The body was a cage, and inside that cage was something which looked, listened, feared, thought and marveled; that something, that remainder left over after the body

---

14   C.f., Robert E. Kirk, "Zombies versus Materialists," *Proceedings of the Aristotelian Society*, 48 (1974): 135–52. C.f., Ludwig Wittgenstein, *Philosophical Investigations*, trans. G. E. M. Anscombe (New York: Macmillan, 1953), 126e (#420).
15   Incredibly, some atheists are quite happy to abolish talk about basic human experiences, c.f. Paul Churchland, whose espoused system of eliminative materialism proposes to do away with notions of "desires, beliefs, fears, perceptions, intentions, and so forth…" "Eliminative Materialism and Propositional Attitudes," *The Journal of Philosophy* 78 (1981): 67–90, 68. When your theoretical system forces you to stop talking about basic human experiences, it's probably time to go hunting for a new theoretical system.

had been accounted for, was the soul.[16]

People Do Immaterial Things

So our experiences go beyond the body, but also *our actions involve more than our bodies*. What Plato was perhaps the first to realize clearly, is that what we do in the case of intellectual knowledge is something inherently immaterial. We can know things that we have not—and in some cases *cannot*—detect with our senses.

For instance, is a hundred-sided geometric figure possible? Sure it is. But how do you know? Have you ever seen one? Probably not. Can you even imagine it in any detail (try to form a picture in your mind of a shape with one hundred sides)? No, you can't. And yet you still know.

Or try this one: could my childhood dog, named Max, breathe underwater? I bet you know the answer. But how do you know? Did you ever meet Max? Did you ever see what he could do? Of course not, but you understand the nature of a dog, which enables you to know things about Max—like that he didn't have gills—without ever needing to make any physical observations.

Here's another one: what's one billion things plus two billion things? Any idea? Right, it's three billion things. Now how do you know that? Did you need to do a physical survey, go into the physics of the situation, ask about the molecular makeup of the things, or about basic forces operating in the region? No. Did you need to physically experience the things in question? No again. So even without seeing, touching, hearing, smelling or tasting these things, you *know* the answer to the question.

Somebody might object at this point that a calculator knows the same thing (i.e., that one billion plus two billion equals three billion). But that's simply not true. A calculator doesn't know anything. It can take input

---

16 Milan Kundera, *The Unbearable Lightness of Being*, trans. Michael Henry Heim (New York: HarperCollins, 1999), 40.

from buttons and yield a certain arrangement of black marks on the screen (which we then interpret as an equation), but the calculator doesn't have any ideas of its own.

This has major implications. Your senses, as we've shown, are how you know the material world. But if you're able to know something that goes beyond your senses, then you're knowing something that goes beyond the material world. You're knowing the immaterial.

Now here's the kicker: *if you are able to know what is immaterial, then you must be immaterial.* Right? How could you connect with the immaterial realm unless you had something immaterial in you? Your senses know material things because your senses lie in the material world (eyes, ears, tongue, etc...). But if your intellect knows immaterial things, it must be because it lies in the immaterial world.

Finally, if we can know things without relying on matter (remember, you don't need to rely on material investigation to know what one billion things plus two billion things is), then it seems very likely that we can *exist* without relying on matter. Our experiences show that there's a part of us that's immaterial, and our knowledge shows that we can know immaterial things. So when our material component goes, we'll still be able to exist immaterially and know immaterially. We'll still be something and we'll still have something to do.

Again, I can really *know* something, even though what I know isn't physical. But if I can really perceive or detect a non-physical reality, if I can connect to that dimension, it must mean that there's something non-physical about me too. But if there's something non-physical about me, then, philosophically speaking, it's reasonable to think that when the physical part of me goes to pieces at death, the intellectual part of me lives on. It's reasonable to presume the mind continues to exist after the death of the body. Which is, of course, the standard view of the vast percentage of humanity for the vast percentage of human history.